The Living Fountain

Remembrances of Quaker Christianity

The Living Fountain

Remembrances of Quaker Christianity

Benjamin Wood

CHRISTIAN ALTERNATIVE
BOOKS

Winchester, UK
Washington, USA

JOHN HUNT PUBLISHING

First published by Christian Alternative Books, 2023
Christian Alternative Books is an imprint of John Hunt Publishing Ltd.,
No. 3 East St., Alresford, Hampshire SO24 9EE, UK
office@jhpbooks.com
www.johnhuntpublishing.com
www.christian-alternative.com

For distributor details and how to order please visit the 'Ordering' section on our website.

Text copyright: Benjamin Wood 2022

ISBN: 978 1 80341 233 7
978 1 80341 234 4 (ebook)
Library of Congress Control Number: 2022935930

A CIP catalogue record for this book is available from the British Library.

Design: Matthew Greenfield

UK: Printed and bound by CPI Group (UK) Ltd, Croydon, CR0 4YY
Printed in North America by CPI GPS partners

We operate a distinctive and ethical publishing philosophy in
all areas of our business, from our global network of authors to
production and worldwide distribution.

Contents

God speaks to each of us as he makes us,
then walks with us silently out of the night.

These are the words we dimly hear:

You, sent out beyond your recall,
go to the limits of your longing.
Embody me.

Flare up like a flame
and make big shadows I can move in.

Let everything happen to you: beauty and terror.
Just keep going. No feeling is final.
Don't let yourself lose me.

Nearby is the country they call life.
You will know it by its seriousness.

(Rainer Marie Rilke, *Book of Hours,* trans. Joanna Macy)

Other Books by Benjamin J. Wood

*The Augustinian Alternative: Religious Skepticism
and the Search for a Liberal Politics,*
ISBN: 9781506432618

Acknowledgements

This book is dedicated to a circle of F/friends who have, over the years, nurtured my religious life and widened my scholarly horizons. My heart-felt thanks goes firstly to a cluster of Quaker mentors and interlocutors; to my doctorial supervisor Rachel Muers, to Ben Pink Dandelion, Rowena Loverance, Janet Scott, Mark Russ, and Rhiannon Grant. Thanks must also go to local Friends at Carlton Hill Meeting House in Leeds for their kindness and generosity. I can never repay all you have given me dear Friends.

I am particularly indebted to the company and encouragement of Robert Keeble, Richard Hawkins, Kate Scott, and Judith Hardaker. I continue to be sustained and upheld by the graced lives of Betsy Randolph-Horn, Lea Keeble, and Anna Needham. May we meet again on that shore where past and future dance.

I would also like to thank companions from other ecclesial pastures, who, in various ways, have given me the inspiration to complete this project. A special mention goes to Ian Tattum of St Barnabas Church, Southfields, University of Lancaster's finest, Roger Haydon Mitchell, and Ann Marie Mealey, formerly of Leeds Trinity University. For his diligence and continued kindness in proofreading the manuscript, I would like to thank Lucas de Winter. Your constructive suggestions and keen eye have helped bring this book to the light of day.

Finally, I would like to offer my deepest thanks to my family, particularly to my husband and best friend, Steve, for his tolerance, patience, and abiding care. As a rule, writers are very difficult people to live with. We can be anxious and morose, sensitive to criticism and prone to wild swings of emotion. But you have endured all this with quiet grace. When the clouds of despondency loomed, you pushed me to carry on. To borrow some words of Auden's, you are *my North, my South, my East and*

West, my working week and my Sunday rest, my noon, my midnight, my talk, my song. Words fail to express my love and gratitude.

Introduction

Living as Friends or Strangers

The Problem of 'Thin' Quakerism

This is what the LORD says: "Stand at the crossroads and look; ask for the ancient paths, ask where the good way is, and walk in it, and you will find rest for your souls." (Jeremiah 6:16)

I began to write this book because of what I feared was being lost within contemporary British Quakerism. Chief among my anxieties was the sense that many Liberal Quaker communities (of which Britain Yearly Meeting is one) have become simply incapable of communicating a collective spiritual story that can glue individual Friends together. This uncomfortable conclusion has been long in the making. When I first entered the Religious Society of Friends in the mid-2000s, I began my worship life as someone who had felt deeply alienated from the Christianity of my Anglican childhood. The ceremonies and prayers of the Sunday service neither spoke to my heart, nor satisfied my intellectual curiosity. I had, like many in their teens and early twenties, explored other religious traditions, (Buddhism, Hinduism, Judaism, and Neo-Paganism most especially). I learnt much from these encounters, and when I entered membership, I believed that these 'universalist' excursions would enrich the already deep sense of Divine presence I felt in gathered worship. And for a time, so they did. But as the years passed, something strange began to happen. I frequently opened the Bible in Meeting and read passages at random. I started to minister about half-forgotten childhood experiences of God, Jesus, and prayer. I assiduously 'spoke Christian' again, despite personal and intellectual reservations.

1

It was almost as if a deep well of water, frozen over by a long frost, was finally beginning to melt, and something liquid and shining was again gushing forth. Initially, this renewed Christian accent was hardly noticed by Friends who sat with me. I'm sure they regarded my decisive shift in language purely as a peculiar outgrowth, entirely explicable according to my Anglican biography. But for me there was much more going on than religious nostalgia. In the course of deep silence, the reality of these old words would strike at my heart. 'Resurrection', 'Salvation', and 'Divine love' were no-longer dogmatic abstracts but living realities that I could feel deep within. The more I prayed and sat through these well-worn words, the more I saw the linkages between my own childhood Christianity and the radical Christ-centred faith of George Fox. It was almost as if my childhood faith was so much sheet music, only able to give me the outlines of something beautiful. Now, with the help of Quaker waiting, I could hear the symphony whole and entire. I started to see the life and vitality in Jesus' teaching because of the way I worshipped among Friends. But the more I recognised this shift in myself, the more I sensed a Friendly indifference to things that seemed to me essential in making sense of this strange thing called 'Quakerism'. How could we tell visitors about Quaker Testimony if we didn't speak first about Jesus, and the Divine Spirit which inspired his life? How could we make sense of who we are as Quakers', without nourishing our Christian roots? Was it not arrogant to assume that only this generation of Post-Christian Quakers had the right answers to religious questions? Perhaps my most shocking turnabout was my increasing discomfort with an aimless celebration of diversity. A diverse community is a beautiful and precious thing. But I began to wonder: What is the Quaker commitment to diversity for? Does it emerge from a deep place of shared understanding? Or is it just a polite way of skating over differences and avoiding conflict?

In the proliferation of Liberal Quaker self-descriptions (Theist, Non-Theist, and Universalist), I sensed not an exhilarating variety but a fraying of Quaker self-understanding. I started to see many of the most attractive features of Liberal Quakerism, its multiplicity, its theological openness, its inclusiveness, as placing hidden costs upon the spiritual unity and internal coherence of the Quaker Way. Chief among the casualties of Quaker modernism are undoubtedly Christian accounts of God, Jesus, and the spiritual life. Christian language, once the bedrock of Quaker speech and practice, is increasingly relegated to one language-option among others in an ever more elastic Society. This stretching of Quaker identity has, I saw, had profound implications. If we no longer have a shared sense of the Light, God, or Christ, what is the basis for Quaker discernment? Does each individual have their own interpretation? And if so, how could it be said that Meetings come to collective Spirit-led decisions? Once, I would have admired such pluralism. Now I shrunk from radical pluralism, seeing the refusal to say definite things to be the mark of a spiritual path that had lost both its uniqueness and its roots. While radical plurality renders contemporary British Friends more tolerant of differences, such tolerance often makes Friends unsympathetic to the notion of a shared Quaker tradition. As Ben Pink Dandelion noted wryly of this fragmentation in his 2014 Swarthmore Lecture: '[The] basis of our testimony is ... more diffuse; that is, our plural theology means we have plural understandings of what we do in the name of Quakerism. Are we committed to peace because of Mosaic law, the teaching of Jesus, because we believe that all life is sacred, or because of Buddhism or humanism?'[1] The point is well-made. We could apply the same observation to God, Jesus, or Membership, and we would be diagnosing the same problem. While it is true that Liberal Friends are frequently eloquent expositors of their personal spiritual journeys, they are often deeply reticent to express shared visions.

But as I started to sketch this thorny critique, I fretted that such a depressing starting point would end by overshadowing the affirming and loving things I wanted to say about the depths of the contemporary Quaker world. Loss and the fear of loss are very powerful emotions, as cultural conservatives will attest. The desire to conserve can drive us towards a deep love for the accumulated treasures of past generations and propel us to revere what is fragile. But such a posture comes with acute dangers. It may tempt us to an unhealthy nostalgia or push us towards an irrational fear of the present. I did not wish to be captured by such pitfalls. Whatever our failings, contemporary British Quakers are a thirsty pilgrim people, joyful in their longing for justice, for peace, and for beauty. I feel blessed to be in such a community of lovers, mystics, and seekers. Even when Friends feel uncertain and muddled about who they are and where they're going, I contend that the shared Quaker commitment to silence calms and guards us. For all our current shortcomings, we are far from a fractured mirror. But our looking glass needs to be scrubbed and polished so that it might better reflect the light. However, in order to remain faithful to such a hopeful task, I realized that any project of Quaker retrieval needed a positive ideal to inoculate it against reaction or spiteful sectarianism. I found such an ideal in Clifford Geertz's classic anthropological study *The Interpretation of Cultures*. At the heart of the book is Geertz' contention that human societies should be understood as organised symbol-systems that shape the aims, imaginations, and desires of participants. When the field anthropologist studies the courtship rituals of a Hindu village in rural India or the birth customs of Māori people in New Zealand, we are encountering webs of meaning, weaved by generations of symbol-users who have sought to ground and circumscribe their world. In deciphering these structures, Geertz claims that anthropologists can follow two paths of explanation, either adopting a 'thin' or 'thick' description. The most obvious hallmarks of 'thin' descriptions are commitments to generality, universalisation, and systematisation. Those who read culture along these lines seek out general principles of organisation through specific examples. An anthropologist so minded is not interested in the details of a particular South Indian marriage-ceremony but wants to know what such activities can tell an observer about the character of human society in general. In this mode of reasoning, grand theory is applied to rites, symbols, and stories, as if from 'above', in an effort to unlock comprehensive structures of social organisation. In this connexion, one thinks of the daring cross-cultural approaches of Mircea Eliade and Claude Lévi-Strauss, who sought (in their different ways) to offer a universally applicable framework for understanding the character and development of human communities. In the Liberal Quaker world, this approach is followed most assiduously by Universalists. In its most extreme form, Quaker Universalism is wholly uninterested in the idiosyncrasies of Friendly faith, (its specific ways of conceptualising peace, theological conviction, or prayer), and instead, is committed to the search for general principles of 'religion' or 'spirituality' which are thought to underlie all particulars. But Geertz has a warning for Universalists of all kinds. So beguiling are the fruits of generalisation that even the most astute observer rarely notices the social object she is studying being subtly obscured by the vagaries of theory. Suddenly, without our notice, we have stopped describing a living, growing, social world, and started transforming everything into hypothetical shapes and straight lines. What was complex and joyfully entangled, we have made blandly uniform. Indeed, says Geertz, to 'set forth symmetrical crystals of significance, purified of the material complexity in which they were located, and then attribute their existence to autogenous principles of order ... is to pretend a science that does not exist and imagine a reality that cannot be found.'[2] How do we reduce the distorting overlay of a universal theory? The answer lies in disinvesting ourselves of straightforward interpretations or single explanations, and instead, committing ourselves to the task of 'painting' a picture that provides space for light, shade, and complexity. This is a 'thick' description, because it eschews universal or conceptual structures, and instead analyses the specific bonds of language, memory, and social action at work in a given community. As Geertz summarises this trajectory:

> A good interpretation of anything — a poem, a person, a history, a ritual, an institution, a society — takes us into the heart of that of which it is the interpretation. When it does not do that, but leads us instead somewhere else — into an admiration of its own elegance, of its author's cleverness, or of the beauties of Euclidean order – it may have its intrinsic charms; but it is something else than what the task [is] at hand...[3]

The analysis of actions alone cannot give us a rich enough picture of the deep 'whys' that lie beneath communal life. In order to truly understand a culture, we must familiarise ourselves with the subtle meanings that suffuse daily social interactions. In an illuminating example of the problem, Geertz notes:

> Consider ... two boys rapidly contracting the eyelids of their right eyes. In one, this is an involuntary twitch; in the other, a conspiratorial signal to a friend. The two movements are, as movements, identical; from an I-am-a-camera, "phenomenalistic" observation of them alone, one could not tell which was twitch and which was wink, or indeed whether both or either was twitch or wink. Yet the difference, however unphotographable, between a twitch and a wink is vast as anyone unfortunate enough to have had the first taken for the second knows. The winker is communicating, and

6

indeed communicating in a quite precise and special way: (1) deliberately, (2) to someone in particular, (3) to impart a particular message, (4) according to a socially established code, and (5) without cognizance of the rest of the company.[4]

Here is the key point. If we wish to understand a culture 'from the inside', we need to comprehend the codes, social niceties, and norms that give particular actions their meaning. Attempting to understand actions without this prerequisite context will lead to unwarranted deductions or mistaken conclusions. Nowhere is this dedication to specificity stronger for Geertz than in the area of religious traditions. A particular preoccupation for Geertz throughout *The Interpretation of Cultures* is demonstrating how sacred symbols 'synthesize a people's ethos – the tone, character, and quality of their life, its moral and aesthetic style and mood and their world view – the picture they have of the way things in sheer actuality are, their most comprehensive ideas of order.'[5] Take for example the practice of sacred silence. The use of waiting/listening silence is common to both unprogrammed Quakers and Zen Buddhists. While on the surface both communities are engaged in essentially the same practice, (some said by many latter-day Quaker Universalists), they in fact emerge from radically different cultural symbol-systems, which direct their users towards different life-projects and priorities. Viewed at the level of generality, Quaker and Zen Buddhist cultures may embrace silent spirituality, but they do so on the basis of different concepts. 'Spirit' and 'Buddhahood' may possess an analogous function within their respective cultural systems, but these concepts (differing as they do in symbolic content), result in separate stories, principles, and preoccupations. In this respect, the ideal anthropologist for Geertz is not merely on the hunt for 'family resemblances' (viewed from outside a particular culture) but desires to enter into the idiosyncratic symbolic systems that induce a 'worshipper to a certain distinctive set of dispositions (tendencies, capacities, propensities, skills, habits, liabilities, pronenesses), which lend a chronic character to the flow of his activity and the quality of his experience.'[6] In place of elegant generalities, we must immerse ourselves in the specifics of a given culture if we wish to understand it. The aim, according to Geertz, should be to gain 'access to the conceptual world in which our subjects live so that we can, in some extended sense of the term, converse with them.'[7]

In this generous commitment, Geertz helped me see the proper trajectory for this book. But instead of studying groups of 'cultural others', my project asks Quakers themselves to recover their own symbol-system from the multiple disrepairs and confusions caused by the universalising power of hyper-Liberalism. What this book implores Friends to do is to sink down into the distinctive words, practices, and symbols, that make us Quaker. In this respect, when one reads *The Interpretation of Cultures* one becomes painfully aware of the present Quaker predicament. With its focus on orthopraxy, universality and personal stories, Liberal Quakerism perhaps resembles the kind of 'thin' description which might be offered by an outsider. We Friends know the kind of things 'Quakers do', but we often lack the symbolic context which might help us understand why we do what we do. As Quaker Liberals, we have held fast to the external world of acts, while forgetting the stories and symbols that give these practices a coherent shared meaning. We have in essence made ourselves strangers to our own Quaker tradition by flattening its content. In presenting the problems of contemporary Liberal Quakerism in this way, I am not advocating a project of cultural isolation or introducing a fundamentalist appeal to 'religious purity'. As Geertz would doubtless remind us, symbol-systems are not hermetically sealed unities. Internally, there may be substantial disagreement about the meaning of particular symbols and practices. Externally, cultures and traditions are in a constant state of dialogue and negotiation as they encounter 'social others'. This means that it is perfectly possible for the Zen Buddhist to cross the cultural threshold into the Quaker symbol system and find common ground, and even carry Quaker co-ordinates with him, adding them in time to his own symbol-system. The same is true in the Quaker case. But we should not ignore the fact that each system coheres according to distinctive rules (one might say grammars) that differ one from another. Evidence of the differences between symbolic systems is vividly furnished by the case of the hybrid-user, who is able to 'converse' through more than one symbolic system. We know from experience that the Quaker-Buddhist is not a grammatical impossibility, but know too that the component parts of the description do not immediately 'fit together'. To make such a dual identity stable, the co-symbolist needs to display the capacity for creative negotiation, reinterpretation, and translation. These practices of fusion acknowledge tacitly that for all the possible overlaps between cultural orders, there are irreducible differences that make the words 'Quaker' and 'Buddhist' intelligible. If all traditions or spiritualities are 'deep down' the same, such creative stitching would never be needed. By identifying the divergences between 'Quaker' and 'Buddhist' worldviews say, I am not attempting to make any exclusivist claims about the ultimate incompatibility of differing worldviews, nor the relative merits of separate symbol-systems. My object is simply to draw attention to the fact that the differences between cultures are just as important in their proper interpretation as their apparent similarities. If we take this starting point seriously, an urgent task naturally presents itself. How do we rediscover the habit of offering a 'thick' description of Quaker speech and action? What essential fragments of context do we need to make sense of our own Quaker actions and symbols? In this book, I will suggest interlocking forms of recovery, from the re-affirmation of Quaker God-language to a renewed appreciation of Christ-talk. But, using Geertz as provocation, it might be asked what deep structures draw these themes together?

Light and Darkness: A Window into the Quaker Worldview

[T]hink of Adam and Eve like an imaginary number, like the square root of minus one: you can never see any concrete proof that it exists, but if you include it in your equations, you can calculate all manner of things that couldn't be imagined without it. (Philip Pullman)

At the risk of pre-empting the substantive arguments of this book, a few things should be said in advance about a distinctly Quaker worldview in order to set the tone for the pages that follow. Perhaps the easiest way into the Quaker symbol system is to consider the repeated dualism between Light and Darkness in early Friends' exposition of their faith. The essence of this early preaching is still very much with us. Nestled in the cherished pages of *Advices and Queries*, we find the following lines: 'Take heed, dear Friends, to the promptings of love and truth in your hearts. Trust them as the leadings of God whose Light shows us our darkness and brings us to new life' (QF&P 1.02.1). This progression from darkness to light is an ancient symbolic motif, found in countless myths and heroic tales. From *Beowulf* to Dante's *Divine Comedy*, from *Gilgamesh* to *Star Wars*, this contest has sculpted and inspired both civilizations and intrepid personalities. In the perpetual struggle between two irreconcilable realms, whole cultures have sought to rise to the dual challenges of valour and spiritual perfection. From this cross-cultural vantage-point Quakerism is no different.

In the testimony of early Friends, the dimension of spiritual darkness was understood as both a ubiquitous force and a personal reality. In the latter aspect, the darkness frequently wore horrifying faces. Early Friends frequently spoke of 'the devil's works'[8] that oppressed a once pure creation. Such repression not merely included the chilling possibilities of demonic possession and witchcraft, but the inexplicable acts of brutality and deception that habitually defaced the world. As James Nayler expressed this latter dimension of spiritual darkness in his 1657 tract *The Lamb's War:*

> The Lamb's quarrel is not against the creation, for then should his weapons be carnal, as the weapons of the worldly spirits are: "For we war not with flesh and blood," nor against the creation of God; that we love; but we fight against the spiritual powers of wickedness, which wars against God in the creation, and captivates the creation into the lust which wars against the soul, and that the creature may be delivered into its liberty prepared for the sons of God. And this is not against love, nor everlasting peace, but that without which can be no true love nor lasting peace.[9]

As Nayler's pamphlet testifies, Friends often felt themselves in combat in ways that far transcended the bloody civil wars that blighted their world. Bloodshed was grievous and evil, but it was a mere symptom of a world that had been mastered by an ancient malevolence. But alongside this highly personalist language of evil, Friends frequently imagined spiritual darkness in ways that were far more structural and pervasive in character. In the minds of early Quaker polemicists, darkness stuck to people and things like treacle, affecting brutality and hatred wherever it settled. It covered the hands of unscrupulous landlords; it clung to the skin of hateful magistrates and prideful monarchs. It was drawn towards the glitter of money and the hollow glory of extravagance. It suffused churches and palaces, homes, and hovels. It even infected the world of nature through disordered human motives. Thus, Edward Burrough lamented in 1661:

> And (man) being possessed with evil and corrupted, he makes all creatures evil in his exercise of them, and he corrupts them and perverts them to another end than wherefore they were created ... and they become a curse unto man and not a blessing, though in themselves are neither cursed, nor evil, nor defiled ... and ruling over them in oppression and cruelty and hard-heartedness, and not in the wisdom of God ... and this ought not to be for it is out of the covenant of God, in which all creatures were made, and in which all stand, except the creature man, who degenerated out of God's covenant.[10]

In Burrough's description, we arrive at the heart of the matter. What early Friends understood as 'darkness' was not merely concerned with individual wrongdoing, but referred to a collective state, of being *out of joint* with the divine order of the universe. All the habits that are commonly called 'sins' among religious moralists were just secondary expressions of a more general condition of estrangement between God and creation. But in conveying a condition of fracture both wide and deep, early Friends, like all Christians before them, touched upon a profound mystery. Where did spiritual darkness come from? Following their Christian forebears, Friends located the source of this all-suffusing evil in an everlasting past that anthropologists call *myth*. In our post-Enlightenment world 'the mythic' has taken on connotations of falsehood or childish fable. But in pre-modern societies myths signified stories about events that are indescribably distant from the present, and yet are still happening. For early Friends, Adam and Eve were not merely personages, they were natures that revealed how evil entered

12

into the world and distorted it. In the deceit of the serpent and the shame of Adam, Fox discerned the essence of sin; the refusal to submit to the truth in oneself. Sin is the primary lie that a creature can exist independently from the Life and Spirit which gives all beings their existence. As Fox wrote in an epistle of 1679:

> And the serpent's false doctrine and teaching was, "Ye shall not surely die if ye eat. thereof, but your eyes shall be opened, and ye shall be as gods," & c. So here was the first false doctrine taught by the world's god, who is out of truth, who was a liar from the beginning, and a murderer, who taught that doctrine contrary to the Lord God, which by feeding on it, and obeying his voice, brought man and woman into the death and fall, from the image of God, and to himself, who abode not in truth.[11]

In this act of separation says Fox, 'the ear went from the Lord's voice and command, after the serpent's doctrine; and the eye went out from the Lord, and after that the mouth went also'.[12] This process of departure culminates in a natural order utterly hostile to human interests, and the intrusion of death into the world. What shall we make of this picture? In a world after Darwin, we find it nearly impossible to link the Fall to anything like history. Consequently, whatever the spiritual insights embedded in the loss of Eden, we habitually regard the story precisely in the way the Enlightenment has trained us, as merely an idle fable. The suggestion that this Iron Age creation story tells us anything about our cosmic situation is met by most with absolute bafflement. But as Fox himself would doubtless remind us, we must not fixate on the outward husk of words. Instead, we must attend to the Spirit that lives within the words of Scripture, and detect, if we can, how they speak to our own condition. The rebellion of Adam and Eve is paradigmatic of an essential situation which is cosmic, social, and existential all at once. A world born from love and joy now finds itself alienated from its source. The Light of God calls to the world like the lover in Solomon's song:

> All night long on my bed
> I looked for the one my heart loves;
> I looked for him but did not find him.
> I will get up now and go about the city,
> through its streets and squares;
> I will search for the one my heart loves.
> So I looked for him but did not find him. (NIV, Song of Songs 3:1–2)

But the world, in its gloom and obliviousness, has forgotten the face of the one it really loves. In the coolness of distance, the world wrangles in grief, fixation, and regret. Poetically speaking, sin is a love affair that has gone cold. Evil is the mirror image of the intimacy of the lovers' arms, alone, aloof, isolated. To talk about 'fallenness' is to name this fundamental failure of love, the failure of social goodness to last, and earthly love to endure. But as Fox would have conceded, when we speak in this way, we are doing nothing less than touching deep mysteries, the answers to which, even Scripture is silent. We do not know the full nature of this cataclysm. Did it happen at a moment in time? Or is time some consequence of its operation? Christian faith is frustratingly ambiguous on these matters. But an account of causes would not help us much, even if we knew them. The important point is that we live in the aftermath of a desolation that now echoes throughout all of history. Life is now marred by death, just as love is distorted by egoism and deceit. Creatures that desire rest are pitted together in an endless struggle for sustenance and survival. This was the received orthodoxy of Christendom that Friends took for granted. But the Quaker symbol-system possessed a radical imminence which set it apart from the other sects of the 1640s. Spiritual Light was not confined to private visions or deathbed consolations, but could be experienced in the exhilarating immediacy of the present. If we held to the spiritual illumination accessible within each heart, we could rise above the powers of darkness, and become vessels of spiritual light.

Quakerism or Living in Paradise

> Yea, I have been in Paradise several days and now I am about to enter eternal happiness. (Quaker martyr Mary Dyer)

As we shall see in this book, early Quakerism was defined by its opposition to otherworldly and despairing tendencies within English Puritanism. While many Puritans quietly waited for God to deliver them from sin at their death, Quakers sought an instant reassurance of restoration in their own lives and hearts. Fox believed that if Friends abided in the Light given to them, they could experience what Scripture garbed in the language of Adam's garden. Instead of enduring an incessant gulf between creatures and Creator, those devoted to the Light in themselves could taste the primordial unity which is the inheritance of all beings. As Fox tells us in his Journal:

> Now I was come up in spirit through the flaming sword, into the paradise of God. All things were new; and all the creation gave unto me another smell than before, beyond what words can utter. I knew nothing but pureness, and innocence, and righteousness; being renewed into the image of God by Christ Jesus, to the state of Adam, which he was in before he fell. The creation was opened to me; and it was showed me how all things had their names given them according to their nature and virtue.[13]

What is Fox trying to tell us here? While the Scriptures taught that the entrance to an earthly Paradise was forever barred (Genesis 3:24) early Quakers saw their devotion to the inward Christ as a means of returning themselves to a state of perfection. The Quaker tradition has always been divided between ecstatic accounts of restoration (the high mystics) and spiritual gradualists (the Augustinians). But Quakerism is unanimous that restoration in time is not merely possible but essential to the meaning of God's Kingdom, as inaugurated in the life, death, and Resurrection of Jesus. When Mary Magdalene weeps in the garden for her dead Lord, she believes she stands in the grove of the fallen world, full of thorns and briers. Nothing grows in this soil except by blood and tears. Weary of life's pain, she asks one she takes to be a gardener: 'Sir, if you have carried him away, tell me where you have put him, and I will get him' (John 20:15). But as she looks into the face of this stranger, she discovers she is no longer in the garden of evil but stands again in the freshness of Eden. Jesus stands before her, injured but whole. For the Magdalene, death and parting has been undone forever. The woundedness of time has been touched by the sweet balm of Eternity. In the garden where death has died, Adam's wounds are finally healed, not in some ethereal after-world, but in history where it all began. Here we touch the essence of a 'thick' Quakerism. Our Meetings are not just benign spaces for individual spiritual projects, but sites of a shared story, rooted in the promise of universal transformation. In this account, we do not sit in silence for ourselves alone, but in the name of a burdened creation which longs to know the Infinite love of God. What then does this story of darkness and light give us as Quakers? Geertz in an illuminating passage suggests:

We are, in sum, incomplete or unfinished animals who complete or finish ourselves through culture — and not through culture in general but through highly particular forms of it.... Man's great capacity for learning, his plasticity, has often been remarked, but what is even more critical is his extreme dependence upon a certain sort of learning: the attainment of concepts, the apprehension and application of specific systems of symbolic meaning. Beavers build dams, birds build nests, bees locate food, baboons organize social groups, and mice mate on the basis of forms of learning that rest predominantly on the instructions encoded in their genes and evoked by appropriate patterns of external stimuli: physical keys inserted into organic locks. But men build dams or shelters, locate food, organize their social groups, or find sexual partners under the guidance of instructions encoded in flow charts and blueprints, hunting lore, moral systems, and aesthetic judgments: conceptual structures molding formless talents.[14]

How then are Friends completed and moulded by the Quaker tradition? Firstly, the stories we tell about ourselves frame us as a non-violent people, who trust a 'God of peace' (Hebrews 13:20). We live not according to might or right, but according to the gracious love we feel in our Worship together. Our Quaker culture completes us by encoding habits of thankfulness, reconciliation, and forgiveness into our daily lives. But these 'formless talents' lead us to a second recognition. As Friends we do not entirely belong to the age, the economy, and the society we are born into. Quakers are not merely a 'culture', we are a counterculture which is often opposed to the dominant ethos we lie within. Our stories about God, love and truth are as beautiful as they are subversive. While many Friends live outwardly ordinary lives, doing ordinary jobs, Friends are at bottom 'sleeper agents', who at any moment could be asked to separate themselves from cosy conformity and speak truth to power. When we sit together in silent waiting, we are continually reminded of our counter-cultural essence. We are invited into a Life of community, service, and mutual healing. When we seek justice and peace, we do so not for the expedient ends of ideological machines, but because we are seeking to liberate a world which is groaning under the grief of estrangement. We do not want to 'win', but to care and bless, cherish, and repair. As a consequence, the Quaker worldview cannot see history simply as a struggle between class-based, racial, or national groups. History begins and ends not with human struggle and human ambition, but with the saving work of God who transcends all human scarcities and barriers. In making such grand claims about what 'Quaker stories' say, I am liable to be stepping on the toes of those who want Quakerism to be a fluid personal doctrine, a private spirituality that eschews the grandness, and possible dogmatism, of a worldview. To such Friends, I can only reply that this book's sense of a shared Quaker vision does not negate individual interpretations of spiritual life, but it does place these personal stories into a shared narrative. It assumes only that Quakerism has a character and an essence, which sustains and shapes those who live within it. But if some Friends are seeking an authoritarian dissection of 'right' and 'wrong' Quakerisms (a modern iteration of 'back to Barclay'), I hope such Friends will be equally disappointed. My object in the following chapters is not to attack Friends who do not agree with me but offer a framework through which we can better cherish our shared Quaker tradition. It is hoped that love and not conformity has been the guiding impetus of this book.

1

Liberal Quakerism: Stories Lost and Found

Who Are We?

A few days before Britain Yearly Meeting 2018, a comment piece appeared in Britain's *Guardian* newspaper with the mischievous title, 'The Quakers are right. We don't need God' (May 4, 2018). The piece's author, Simon Jenkins, praised British Friends for their refreshing take on spiritual matters:

> The Quakers are clearly on to something. At their annual get-together this weekend they are reportedly thinking of dropping God from their "guidance to meetings". The reason, said one of them, is because the term "makes some Quakers feel uncomfortable". Atheists, according to a Birmingham University academic, comprise a rising 14% of professed Quakers, while a full 43% felt "unable to profess a belief in God". They come to meetings for fellowship, rather than for higher guidance.[15]

Instead of taking refuge in metaphysical consolations, Jenkins sees Quakers as a group of honest therapeutics, committed to 'expressing doubts, fears and joys amid a company of "friends", who respond only with their private silence.'[16] Suffice to say, Jenkins' interpretation of contemporary British Quakerism generated a forceful response in the letters' page of the *Guardian*, with one Friend remarking, 'discomfort with "God language" is not the same thing as the abandonment of a spiritual life. Even non-theist Quakers have a spiritual life, and certainly don't come to meetings just for fellowship.' Another Friend remarked, 'While there is certainly a spectrum of beliefs among Quakers, including those who call themselves "non-theists", the question is more to do with how Friends think of God than of his absence.'[17] While these responses are clearly meant to reassure the reader that Liberal British Quakerism has not become a form of secular therapy, the clear acknowledgement of discomfort with theological language and the recognised existence of a 'spectrum of beliefs', is indicative of an unruly complexity at the heart of British Quakerism. But such diversity is not simply disconcerting to outsiders like journalists but has long been puzzling to Friends themselves. As Keith Redfern expressed this predicament in the late 1990s:

The current climate is one of questioning and self-examination in an effort to find the right way forward. Before we can do this however, we have to be sure that we know who we are. Although British Quakers maybe clear individually as to their stage on a spiritual journey, as a religious community it seems that we are still seeking unity regarding our overall spiritual position.[18]

At the forefront of such soul-searching are a wide-ranging set of questions concerning what constitutes central Quaker beliefs, the justification of Friends' historical practices of peace and discernment, and the ongoing basis for Quaker community and corporate witness. But alongside such existential queries, an increasing number of Friends are content with the open-ended reality of radical diversity. It has been suggested, not least by the Non-Theist Quaker writer David Boulton, that seeking Redfern's 'overall spiritual position' might be an impractical red herring. As an alternative to seeking out a unified Quaker perspective, Boulton is much more concerned with practical matters of co-existence and mutual affirmation. Instead of seeking to answer the thorny question 'what are Quakers doing when they sit in silence?', Boulton is satisfied with the simple empirical reality of internal Quaker elasticity. As Boulton summarises this self-consciously inclusive viewpoint:

> The theological diversity that has increasingly marked liberal Friends throughout the world over the last 120 years is the result of our growing discernment that unity is not dependent on someone's notion of doctrinal orthodoxy. That's a liberating experience – and a humbling one! It has freed us up to think and rethink everything, to challenge ourselves and each other. There's nothing incoherent about accepting that we don't know it all, about living the questions rather than insisting that we have all the answers. It means recognising that Quakers are still seekers on a continuing journey, not finders at the end of the road.[19]

But there is a weakness in Boulton's tender empiricism. To say that one is on a continuing journey, rather than a careless roam, suggests a general direction of travel and a final destination. But diversity is a fact, it is neither a direction nor a destination. To treat diversity as a trajectory merely sidesteps the very real problems of sustaining intelligibility and belonging. Even 'being different together' must involve a degree of shared meaning, understanding, or expectations. The tensions produced by self-justifying diversity become acutely visible when Friends are asked to explain what they are doing in Meetings for Worship for Business. Is the Meeting's practice of discernment dependent upon a conception of Divine Guidance? Or is Church government a form of consensus decision-making, drawing upon the unconscious wisdom of the group? So much of what we think 'being Quaker is', hangs on the answer we give to this kind of first order question. If the former interpretation prevails among Friends present, the decision arrived at will be understood as possessing a possible significance far beyond the preoccupations of those gathered. To say that God is glimpsed in 'the sense of the Meeting' tells us something key about the nature of God and the nature of Meeting. In this account of Worship, the Spirit dwells in and alongside the decisions we make. Here Friends are not individual operators deciding between competing options, but seekers after an abiding Truth in every situation. Moreover, the God at the centre of the discernment process is active, willing, and desiring *something for us*. Even a relatively mundane decision concerning repairs on the Meeting House roof is treated as potentially illustrative of God's ongoing presence in the life of a given Quaker community. If the latter interpretation is taken as normative, however, the decision a Meeting reaches simply reflects contingent circumstances and cannot be expected to carry any deeper significance beyond the meaning or synchronicity it has for those present.

For a Non-Theist, for whom 'God' is a useful metaphor for human goodness, or for a Universalist, who regards 'God' as characterless 'Spirit', 'energy' or 'spiritual essence', the notion of following a distinct Will in Worship dissolves into incomprehensibility. In this psychological guise, discernment practice can neither illuminate the ultimate ends a group might take, nor tell us anything specific about the substance of the words 'God' or 'discernment' that are purportedly at the heart of the exercise. Disagreement over the meaning of such a foundational practice, suggests at the very least a tension between a human-centred account of Worship and one which assumes the activity of a non-human yet desiring dimension which works in, but does not belong to, a group's immediate conditions. The difference is thus not just about propositions, but one's orientation towards life, meaning, and Quaker Worship. While such differences of approach need not spill over into conflict, they are potentially destabilising, especially when Worship brings contentious issues to the surface. When we seek the right way forward in Meeting, are we led by an imperative beyond ourselves? Or is our task to adequately 'represent' the individual perspectives of the group? Put in this way, the divisions of understanding between Friends in a single Meeting could be stark and lead to significantly different outcomes. A gathering based on a democratic ethos of consensus or buying-off competing interests, is quite different from one that sees its task as divining a will not wholly its own. As Redfern notes:

> We are a Religious Society, in direct descent from those of the 17th century who realised that it is possible to have a direct communication with God; that we are not alone in our decision making, but that the Spirit is constantly on hand to guide and advise. If we insist on going it alone in our Quaker business, we may never find unity in anything and risk pulling our Yearly Meeting asunder.[20]

One does not have to wholly agree with Redfern's catastrophic conclusion to see the fundamental issue at stake. If radical diversity constitutes the essential reality of contemporary British Quakerism, the question rightly persists, what, if anything, unites its miscellaneous strands? Does the Spirit evoked in the process of Quaker discernment even have an identifiable character to which disparate Quakers can assent? My central purpose in this chapter is not to provide definitive answers to all these questions. Rather, I want to consider why these questions are being asked in the first place, and the environment which has produced them. Once this context has been established, I seek to show the recurrent weaknesses of some of the most common answers Friends offer in the face of our multiplicity. My purpose in such dissections is to move discussions of Quaker identity away from the quagmire of diversity and towards a shared conception of 'being' and 'living' Quaker.

To ground the latter task, the first part of this discussion offers a short historical analysis of Liberal Quakerism through the work of the American scholar of Religion Rufus Jones (1863–

1948). Of particular concern for Jones was rooting Friends' history and practice within the framework of a cosmopolitan and epoch-crossing mysticism, capable of uniting diverse cultures and creeds. At the heart of this venture, was Jones' audacious reframing of the early Quaker doctrine of the 'Inward Light' in ways that amplified human power and dignity. While early Friends had defined the Inward Light as God's judgement on and within the conscience, Jones understood this foundational Quaker tenet as signifying nothing less than a fundamental alignment between the human self and Godself. The Light was not merely a communication of God, but a way of speaking about an inherent divine spark in everyone. Closely echoing the creative preoccupations of the Romantics, Jones goes on to suggest that the imaginative power of the divine life is interwoven and co-determinant with both human consciousness and creativity. In this anthropology, human personality was both divinely stamped and, Godself, utterly transcendent. As we shall see, such a close identification between God and Self had radical consequences for the development of Quaker Liberal Theology. While Jones was keen to stress his resistance to both solipsism and egotism, such an exaggerated conception of near-divine selfhood provided a fertile soil for an increasingly disparate and diversifying Quakerism which looked ever more inward for its validation. If consciousness expressed one's inward divinity, then one's choices became extensions of revelation. Under the sway of such permissive mysticism, Meeting for Worship could be reimagined as a vast umbrella under which a variety of beliefs could be grown and fostered. What were the consequences of Jones' reconfiguration of Quaker identity? In the second part of this chapter, I consider both the gifts and costs of Jones' refashioning of Quaker self-understanding. While Romantic mysticism enabled Liberal Friends to respond with loving welcome to new multicultural and interreligious realities, such liberality often came at the price of neglecting distinctive elements of Quaker speech and story. In the Liberal Quaker eagerness to respond to the cultural and scientific transformations of modernity, Liberal Quaker theology absorbed many of the modern world's hubristic and solipsistic tendencies, without submitting them to critical interrogation. This created conditions for a new mode of Quaker selfhood which regarded spirituality as a private possession, one which could be defined and redefined at will. As a counter to this rather atomistic conception of the religious life, the final part of this chapter argues for the reassertion of a shared Quaker story that takes as its starting point our common history and religious language. While by no means seeking to impose an orthodoxy upon Friends, such a project is intended to show how we can better be Quakers together, sustained by a substantial narrative that does not refute our diversity, but rather frames and orders it.

The Romantic Quakerism of Rufus Jones

Rufus Jones remains one of the most influential articulators of liberal-modernist Quakerism. A guiding impulse of Jones' scholarly work was the elucidation of the concept of mysticism and its relation to Quaker History and Worship. This project proved powerful midst the manifold social upheavals of the late nineteenth and early twentieth century. As William James had suggested in his 1902 study *The Varieties of Religious Experience*, one could now study religious belief in ways that cut across the peculiarities of culture and doctrine, and instead encourage often jaded Western believers to adopt an expansive psychological and non-literal appreciation of religious ideas and forms. In this mode of analysis, the feelings evoked by Notre Dame Cathedral, Bach's St Matthew's Passion, or the Golden Temple at Amritsar, were just as important as the finer points of ritual purification or theology. For James, this new lens was called 'mysticism'. The core of this label rested on the claim that the coherence of religion did not ultimately depend upon complex theologies, but upon the direct experience of each believer. But for psychological inquirers into these religious states, it was possible to glimpse social implications far beyond the merely academic. As the theologian Peter Tyler notes concerning the potency of this mystical turn, to postulate a personal and inward form of religious life was to imagine something 'liberal and universal without being dogmatic, ecclesiastical, sacramental, or sectarian'.[21]

In an age after absolute authority and unquestioned religious belonging, mysticism offered a new glue and a new programme for disparate religious communities seeking to make sense of the modern world. In this progressive spirit, Jones claimed a perennial core to Quakerism, which transcended theological lexicons, geography, or particular practices. This secured for progressive British and American Friends potent new ways of thinking about their faith in a scientific and multireligious age. While externally, the Religious Society of Friends constituted a peculiar outgrowth of sectarian Puritanism, at the level of abiding substance, Quakerism expressed for Jones the shared human stirring for divine immediacy. As Jones summarised the tone of this project in his 1923 *Studies in Mystical Religion*:

> There have been religious geniuses in all ages and in all countries who have had experiences of spiritual expansion. They have been made aware of a Realm of reality on a higher level than that revealed through their senses. They have sometimes felt invaded by the inrush of a larger Life; sometimes they have seemed to push a door inward into a larger range of being with a vastly heightened energy. The experience is ... always one of joy and rapture; in fact it is probably the highest joy a mortal can feel.[22]

In chronicling these exalted experiences, Jones saw Friends' distinctive mission as 'mystical and prophetic'; a body of believers that should be judged not according to doctrines or habits but 'by the way it has been an organ of the Spirit'.[23] Universal personal revelation, not particulars, animate what is most essential for Jones in the Quaker Way. In positing an inward religion of mystical experience as primary, Jones had several outstanding preoccupations. The first was to link the unity-seeking self of mystical excursion to the creative Romantic individualism of early modernity.[24] By extending the range of mystical sources to include contemporary figures, Jones sought to show a basic sympathy between the striving contemplative and the restless souls of modern democratic civilization. In seeking to expand the category of 'mystical experience', Jones mined artists and poets for a keener expression of the Ultimate. One of Jones' guiding assets in this endeavour were the New England Transcendentalists. With their combined interests in individual self-expression and a Vedantic over-soul,[25] writers such as Thoreau and Emerson, offered a Quaker Liberal such as Jones a compelling conduit between archaic wisdom and contemporary conditions. The most significant impact of such synthesis was Jones' radical reconfiguration of the early Quaker doctrine of the Inward Light. For early Friends, the Inward Light signified the presence of God in the innermost conscience and, at the centre of this conception, was the declaration of Paul in Romans:

> Indeed, when Gentiles, who do not have the law, do by nature things required by the law, they are a law for themselves, even though they do not have the law. They show that the requirements of the law are written on their hearts, their consciences also bearing witness, and their thoughts sometimes accusing them and at other times even defending them... This will take place on the day when God judges

people's secrets through Jesus Christ, as my gospel declares.
(NIV, Romans 2:14–16)

In this passage, Friends found reflected their sense of a God
who broke open their lives to the core. They knew themselves
under a law that accused them of complacency, lust, and
hypocrisy. To be under the guidance of the Light was firstly
to be confronted with a charge sheet. As the early Quaker
William Shewen expressed this experience in his short treatise
Concerning Thoughts and Imagination:

> Now it is a heavenly state to live under the government of
> Christ, to know and experience him, swaying the sceptre of
> the heart, and established in the throne thereof. But none
> come to enjoy this, till they have first known him to sit as
> a refiner with fire and a fuller with soap, and as a spirit
> of judgement and burning, and as the stronger man to
> dispossess the strong man, spoil all his goods and sweep and
> cleanse the house....[26]

Thus for early Quakers, the journey into the Light began with
the recognition of a duplicitous and obstinate self, a being who
naturally resisted the call to deep love and transformative grace.
But if an experience of the Light meant being placed under
judgement, the same Light defended the self by promising
its final restitution through a direct apprehension of the love
of God. While the implications of such inward conversion
were radical, the basic pattern from sin to regeneration was
recognisably Puritan in character. Like other dissenting sects
of the period, early Friends needed to feel the security of God's
salvation in their bones. Neither theology nor second-hand
opinion could satisfy this need. But such a conception possessed
a gloom and narrowness which sat uneasily with Jones' Mystical
and modernist inclinations. Throwing off the last vestiges of a

Puritan religious atmosphere of an older Quaker legacy, Jones insisted instead that the Light was none other than the inherent divine presence in each human being. The God experienced as the Light was no longer the Christ of biblical witness, with a particular story and identity, but a universal force of unity and affirmation that both subsisted in and transcended specific religious claims. Its task was not salvation understood in the traditional senses of that word, but the expansion of human potential and possibility. As Jones reflected in his introduction to Braithwaite's *The Beginnings of Quakerism*, the inward light doctrine signified an attempt to:

> restore individual responsibility, spiritual initiative, and personal autonomy. Man himself with his inherent divine rights and his eternal destiny is put in the place of sacred and time-honoured systems. Whatever hampers, limits restrains, spoils human powers, is to go down at all costs in life, and suffering, and whatever enlarges and liberates and lifts man has a place in the programme of these "Children of the Light".[27]

As the words 'rights' and 'autonomy' indicate, this is not a description of first-generation Quaker sentiment, but an attempt to find in the original language of Quakerism the glimmer of a decidedly modern project, which places human individuality and its powers at the centre of the religious experience. This novel description of early Quakerism as a species of religious humanism reveals a second key preoccupation of Jones' theology, namely the connexion between the inherently divine dimension of human beings and their capacities for imagination and creativity. For Jones, the Transcendentalists had illustrated that mysticism was not merely the passive receipt of Divine Wisdom, but always artistic and affective in its impact. The personality that is swept up in the experience of mystic unity is always invited to an imaginative task of personal expression and outpouring. This focus upon matters of artistic sensibility encouraged Jones to disregard orthodox ontological separations between human and divine action, and instead stress the deep analogies between human and divine creativity. As Jones expresses this identification:

> We carry in the form and structure of our inner selves the mark and badge and lineage and kinship with a realm that can best be called the Eternal, since it is real in its own essential being and of the same nature as God who is the centre of its life and ours.[28]

Going further, Jones even offers his own version of Descartes' famous *cogito* formula in order to establish the spiritual nature of human consciousness. As Jones puts it:

> His [the mystic's] approach to reality is ... not through rocks and hills and skies, and not through molecular forces and the energy of suns, not even through the sacred Himalayas, but through the reality which reaches the highest degree of certainty to him, the reality of his own mind. He begins thus, not with books and documents, not with traditions and external authorities but with the verity of conscious self-existence. The surest evidence that the universe culminates in a type of reality that can be called "spiritual" is to be found in the fact that when we penetrate the labyrinthine ways of our own mind we are already in the realm of spirit.[29]

This exaggerated subjectivism had considerable implications for Jones' understanding of both cultural production and aesthetics. If the inner domain of consciousness is part of the spiritual world, when human beings strive to create something from the recesses of their imaginations, they discover something of the divine within themselves. The implication is that the human production of beauty is an extension of, and co-terminus with, divine creativity. Conjoined with Jones' Romantic theology of co-creation was a third preoccupation, the de-secularisation of human life. Like his Romantic predecessors, Jones attempted to cultivate a deep appreciation of the natural world as a shield against the tendency to reduce everything to a mere object of calculation.[30] Standing against this shallow spirit of commercialism, Jones argued that the apprehension of beauty was capable of inducting us into deeper and more abiding spiritual values. As his voluminous writings show, Jones possessed a keen appreciation of the religious language and metaphysics of William Wordsworth.[31] In conscious imitation of the latter, Jones found in earth, sky, and seasons, a confirmation of divine goodness.[32] But if Jones shared the general healthy-mindedness and optimism of the Romantics, he also displays the Romantic appeal to individuality and radical inwardness, co-equal buttresses against the rigidities and conventions of the world. This manifests most markedly in Jones' anxieties concerning the sacrilegious effects of Enlightenment rationalism and Darwinian Naturalism on the spiritual description of human experience. Despite his sense of ordinary life's sacredness, in the face of profound irreligion, Jones seeks to separate human beings from the temporal world and into a realm of transcendence. In an effort to define the person against the grain of scientific materialism, Jones seeks to demarcate the bodily nature of human beings from their essential non-material essence. This spiritual quality is defined by Jones as that which 'unifies, organizes and interprets everything presented to it'.[33] It is identical with the words 'mind', 'consciousness', and 'soul', containing within itself the capacity to see the invisible structure of the world under the mundane order of things. While this inner self is affected by the character of outer experience, its essence is altogether different from the world it surveys. There is, says Jones, 'nothing outside itself which can explain it', it is unique and 'belongs to a different order'[34] While Jones is at pains to insist that this Deep Self 'is not a spectator mind',[35] the radical turn inward introduces us to the cardinal tension at the heart of Jones' conception of Liberal Quakerism. Despite Jones assertion of a world-engaged 'affirmative mysticism',[36] his attempts to preserve the spiritual self from the brutalising currents of secular modernity, leaves the human person, in its deepest essence, radically separate from the world. Despite Jones' warning against 'the lonely track of egoism'[37] implicit in this notion of the artistic soul is a form of privatised self-making, an orientation which regards external facts as unimportant contingencies that must be transcended in the name of higher purposes. As Jones summarises this impulse:

> Where can God be found? Not in our world of sense anywhere, answers the mystic. Every possible object in our world is a mere finite appearance. It may be as huge as the sun or even the Milky Way, or as minute as the dust speck in the sunbeam; it makes no difference. It is a form of the finite. It is in contrast to the Absolute an illusion, a thing of unreality. It cannot show God or take you to him.[38]

The flipside of this proposition is obvious. The inward self is the most real thing in the world, the most solid object, other than God Himself. We might call the terminus of this position, the mysticism of infinite licence, or to use Ben Pink Dandelion's concise term, 'sacro-egoism'.[39] Since the self in its depth is intrinsically bound to the divine, such a being can in theory become its own self-contained universe, guided solely by its own internal sense of divine co-relation. Such a being is free to reinvent itself in any way that its inner promptings incline. In this latter move, we see the embryonic underpinnings of the postmodern posture that Dandelion calls 'Liberal-Liberal Quakerism'.[40] In this mode, the mystic/creative inner self is given complete free rein, as belief is largely 'pluralised, privatised, but also marginalised'.[41] In this latter form, Quakerism increasingly resembles a subjective therapeutic project of self-discovery, spiritual autonomy, and personal authenticity. It is this conception which now constitutes the little discussed, but essential backdrop to so much of contemporary British Quakerism.

Navigating Radical Diversity: Gifts and Pitfalls

What should we make of the model of Liberal mysticism offered by Jones? Such is its imaginative power on generations of Liberal Quakers, that few contemporary British Friends can imagine any other way of being Quaker. The notion of radical diversity is for many Meetings a mark of their deepest identity. The language of 'mysticism' in this context is deeply appealing since it does not bind people to any particular beliefs, set of images, or sacred stories. Instead, such a framework permits people a mode of rich self-discovery which seeks to include, and not flatten varied perspectives and experiences. Today, such axiomatic universalism helps many Quakers, some of whom have been wounded by the exclusivities of other Churches or traditions, to constitute themselves as a loving and sympathetic community of seekers. As Rhiannon Grant has shown in her recent study of Liberal Quaker theology, such Friends are frequently adept at creating their own accounts of the sacred through a process of continuing reinterpretation.. As Grant summarises this attitude:

British Quakers actively celebrate diversity. They may not be sociologically diverse in many ways, but they prize two ways of being which encourage diversity; independence of mind and spiritual seeking. Someone coming to join such a community representing itself thus is expected to be a seeker and not one looking to be told easy answers which might be swallowed whole. The result of this is a community which, since at least the end of the nineteenth century, has been home to a range of theological views.[42]

To sustain such postures, Grant points to habitual Liberal Quaker tendencies to translate, qualify, and pluralise both theological language and the justifications for distinctly Quaker practices. Not only have Liberal Friends many names for God, but often use such multiple nomenclature as a way of expressing both the inadequacy of a single God-language and the primacy of personal experience.[43] Thus says Grant, Liberal Friends are able to 'say something while making clear that there are things they cannot say'.[44] Such a suspension of finality permits not merely a vast degree of theological latitude in communal settings but allows for considerable personalisation of theological speech and understanding. As Grant notes concerning these trajectories: 'An image of God that is sometimes used in British Quaker thought is that of light passing through a crystal or a prism. The image of God as light is a well-established one in Quakerism, drawing originally on the opening passages of John's Gospel ... [Here] God is revealed differently in the life of each individual.'[45] In this pose of maximum flexibility, any shared understanding is assumed to be in a state of continual revision. This posture of the 'absolute perhaps' creates both space for exploration and a creative means of managing communal conflict. Viewed in its own terms, this pluralistic approach to spiritual life is a precious artefact of Jones' mysticism, a monument to tender religious humanism and a significant achievement of late Quaker culture more generally. But we should not let the richness of this model of mutual co-existence deter us from asking tough questions regarding its communal and theological limitations. Its most significant strength is also its greatest weakness. At the centre of Liberal Quakerism is a fluid conception of selfhood which seeks to build community on the basis of difference. A protective wedge is thus created between self and community, permitting individual Friends to develop their own interpretation of

Quaker life. But if Quaker Liberalism is indeed premised upon a metaphorical distance between group and self, this gulf may prevent some Friends from forming a keener sense of togetherness. Indeed, it is easier in such an environment to go one's own way, turning to the community only when one's inner interpretative resources give out. Considered pragmatically, there is much to be said for not having one's toes stepped on. But we must be under no illusion, such a strategy is not suited for the formation of a cohesive community. Like most philosophies of autonomy, Liberal Friends' methods of appreciating multiplicity are acutely honed to maintain forms of practical equilibrium but have few resources for developing notions of shared stories, experiences, or symbols. This outcome is encoded in the very egoistical inwardness of Jones' mysticism. In the first place, any absolute identification with personal experience may encourage an individual to treat their subjective encounters as the most authentic thing about them. Such a character may regard any intrusion upon that precious feeling of self-discovery as a violation of individual rights or independence. In this account, the notion of any 'given' shared understanding becomes an obstacle to the integrity of one's own spiritual journey. Something of this attitude is expressed by the Universalist Quaker Tony Philpott in his *From Christian to Quaker: A Spiritual Journey from Evangelical Christian to Universalist Quaker*. Part memoir, part defence of Liberal Universalism, Philpott suggests that the great strength of contemporary British Quakerism is its capacity to contain the diverse personal philosophical and spiritual models of its members. Speaking of his own sense of liberation, Philpott writes:

> The freedom to believe what I wish also enables me to use whatever model of the self is appropriate; I am not constrained by the Christian model of 'sinful man' or an atheist model of monism and materialism. As with many of my beliefs I can

have a universalist and syncretic view of the self.[46]

In this type of spiritual life, ultimate authority rests within an enclosed self, one which holds the power to choose the mode of religious relation under which s/he will live. There is little in this perspective that is either unlooked for, or unplanned, with the reflective mind in the driving-seat in selecting all religious stories and symbols. Licenced by the latitude of 'the absolute perhaps', all claims to general spiritual truth become so many private models, an arrangement which is mutually sustained by an atmosphere of 'respect for the individual'.[47] The substance of this approach is recognisably Jonesian. We may all be united by mystical experiences, but these are private revelations, for us to interpret alone. Communities may aid this personal process, but they must never intrude upon the content of our inner experience, which is ours and belongs to no other. As Philpott has defined this commitment to autonomy:

> As I walk down to meeting for worship on a Sunday morning I pass several churches and the cathedral and sometimes I hear the singing of hymns. I also hear the grand sound of bells of the cathedral or the single bell of other churches, ringing out and demanding attendance at their services of worship. All these places blast out authority at the worshipper; hymns, prayers, the sermons, the Bible, God. The 'me' does not get a look in. It was the contrast that Quakers offered to this that stuck with me... I was attending an activity concentrating on spiritual matters, but I was free to think of anything! Even when there was ministry, all I had to do was listen; I didn't even have to say 'Amen'. All I had to do was keep silent and shake hands with the person near to me at the end.[48]

Here silent worship is constructed as a place for personal contemplation and immediate encounter, which need not be connected to a wider sense of belonging or assent. In this description nothing in particular is demanded of us, no specific act of will or giving-over is required. The sense of discipline concerns the outward action only, with the final meaning of the activity left indeterminate. We are permitted to make of the silence what we will. Worship is thus a kind of canvas which waits for us to add our paint brush. Before we wax lyrical about the generosity of such a model, one should be clear about what such a conception of religious life cannot do. It cannot speak collectively of what Quakers *have found*. It cannot say with any definitiveness what belongs to the realm of personal insight and what belongs properly to the group. Indeed, under the dispensation just described, it is questionable that one would wish to make any distinction between individual or collective insight. Both are of the same quality and importance and are in any case the product of co-equal and co-authoritative individuals. True enough, notes Philpott, Liberal Quakers are guided by 'values' which can be identified with Quaker Testimony.[49] These provide definition in an otherwise free-forming group of seekers.[50] But despite this minimal appeal to that which is shared, the goal of Quaker Liberalism is not to maintain community, but rather sustain the integrity of the self. But as Philpott's mention of atheistic materialism intimates, a second ultra-secular course is also possible within the confines of Jones' mysticism. Instead of understanding the personality as an expression of spiritual power, the solipsistic ego may begin to regard itself as the source of all meaning and purpose, including the sensation of transcendence. In its most extreme form, this perspective terminates in the Self becoming all, both God and worshipper, interpreter and meaning giver. Framing this transition to the self through the language of Blakean mysticism, Boulton reflects:

Blake summarises the history of religion in a single short and brilliant passage. The spirits, or gods, or geniuses are not real entities: they were created by the poetic imagination. (When asked where his visions came from, Blake tapped his forehead.) But priesthoods arose to "enslave the vulgar" by stealing the spirits from the poets and artists who made them, building contrived forms of worship around them, and pretending that the gods they had stolen and conscripted to their purpose had themselves "order'd such things". "Thus men forgot that all deities reside in the human breast", the human creative imagination.[51]

Thus, when Boulton attends Meeting he says that he does indeed worship God, 'understanding God as the symbol and imagined personification of mercy, pity, peace, and love ... values which, though they can hardly be anything other than wholly human in origin and expression' are treated by Boulton as if 'they were absolute and transcendent.'[52] Here we see the last outgrowth of Jones' mysticism, the enfoldment of all conceptions of religious life into the immediacy of a choosing self. This final shift also completes our picture of Quaker liberalism more generally. From the single fountain of Jones' mysticism emerges two of the most visible roads of contemporary British Quakerism, Quaker Universalism and Quaker Non-Theism. Despite their significant differences of emphasis, both depend upon a near-identical religious anthropology: that of a self-contained chooser who identifies his preferences with the things that Quaker language has historically regarded as holy, sublime, or ultimate. Having identified and defined this conception, the question arises: Are we content as Quakers with such a self-involved model of spiritual community? Is our Worship together merely a place for an isolated self to assert its life-choices? Or is our silence concerned with the encounter of the self with an unchosen, unlooked-for Other? The choice is no mere theoretical consideration, for our response to this issue decides whether our foundational notions of Quaker discernment, Worship and Spirit-led life have intelligible collective meanings, or whether they are in fact so many contested fragments of largely personal stories. In an effort to ground this second notion of an Other-directed and shared Quakerism, the following discussion argues that alongside the search for personal understanding, Friends should be free to accumulate wisdom, insight, and history. The 'absolute perhaps' should give way to a much more rooted sense of what it means to be Quaker, grounded in a joint conception of a collective Quaker narrative.

The Recovery of Quaker Narrative

In the previous discussion, we saw the way in which Tony Philpott drew the distinction between the freedom of Liberal Quakerism and the demanding authority of other ecclesial traditions. Here authority is conceived of negatively, as that which constrains, forbids, and stifles. In a West living after Locke and Rousseau, this is the unconscious theory of authority that most of us carry around in our minds. We instinctively see authority as standing against personal freedom, creativity, and all-crucial for modern people, the ideal of perfect choice. This habitual 'libertarian' tendency is frequently amplified by the domination of the modern world by corporate standardisation and vast state-organisations. In these enormous undertakings, the individual appears relatively small, unless it concerns a person's preferences in the marketplace. Out of this loss, we pursue forms of consolation that make routinisation bearable. In the midst of the giant bureaucracies that employ us, train us, and standardise our behaviour, we clutch desperately at that which is truly ours, through romance, family life, leisure or cultural escapism. We yearn for things that are safe but unorganised. As far as Liberal Quakerism belongs to this collective psychology, it promises worshippers something like 'religion' without authority. It assures those gathered in a tiny cocoon of private life, uninteresting to our bureaucracies, forms of belonging without stifling order, and sharing without sameness. Thus, it might be said that the anti-authoritarianism of Liberal Quakerism is in part animated by the fear that excessive shared meaning will always become identical with the pushy authorities of the outer world. But this conflation is overly simplistic.

There is another notion of authority, quite alien to our contemporary idea of homogenous order. It is an authority not of pure power, but of cumulative wisdom. Such authority rests on the storehouse of a community's memory, its past attempts to assess insight and dispel error, or the usefulness of beloved practices that solve daily problems. We encounter this kind of authority every day in manifold forms, in the concept of 'local knowledge' or the 'knack' of tying knots, baking bread, placating a toddler, or flipping a pancake. These skills are often social, arising in particular conditions, and perhaps, possessing specific histories. The baker, for instance, when he attempts to perfect his technique, is entering into established traditions. His activities, in the treatment of yeast, or his adoption of an optimum cooking time, both retain, and if he has an apprentice, transmit, certain practices. People who have successfully honed these abilities possess 'authority', not on the basis of power, but on the basis of efficacy or in the case of entertaining a toddler, fluency. This kind of social knowledge is defined less by what it forbids, and more by what it allows users to do. This is the kind of 'authority' Liberal Quakerism needs and habitually resists. So is there a 'knack' to 'being Quaker'? If one is to believe some Liberal Friends, there is extraordinarily little to pass on except general 'Quaker values', and the unwritten rules of Worship, guided by the proviso of the 'absolute perhaps'. But a close study of our book of discipline suggests a different picture, that of a community with a story, with habits, lessons, and local knowledge. As Ben Pink Dandelion has noted:

Our book of discipline embodies and affirms our necessary
commitment to discernment, to seeking always to know.
At the same time, it is a book which, despite its reliance on
outward language, conveys as best we can, our core insights
and our current sense of our spiritual experience in the best
words we have been able to find, discerned by the gathered
meeting, to be of use to us, to provide us with comfort and
with the discomfort of spiritual challenge.[53]

This brings us to a key point. In moments when we are 'gathered',
when we reach the wordless depths, we are more than separate
seekers or self-creators. We are vessels and vehicles, swimming
in a sea of aggregate wisdom. While individual Friends on the
bench may relativise the 'knack' of Quakerism into a series
of personal preferences, our book of discipline reminds us
of a historical narrative that makes coherent, not merely the
generalised 'values' prized by Universalist and Non-Theist
Friends, but more fundamentally, the rationale for our silent
worship and our call to lives of peace. Perhaps most troubling
to Friends inducted into the Universalism of Jones lies primarily
in the fact that Quaker story is structured by the larger imagery
and grammar of the Christian story. This is our indelible core
as Quakers, the soil from which even our most post-religious
expressions spring. If we wish to discover the deep reasons for
our Worship or our peculiar Quaker speech, we must find ways
of rediscovering the Friends who loved and prayed before us.
But in going about such recovery, we should avoid any romantic
suggestion that it is either possible or desirable to simply return
to the past. The arrow of time has one direction only. We are
not seventeenth-century people. We are moderns, with particular
anxieties about the coherence of God-language, the veracity of
faith, and the reliability of religious experience. Unlike early
Friends, we live our lives in mostly secular, largely religiously
plural spaces. Our culture has few if any religious or sacred

givens. To choose a spiritual life often feels like swimming against a heavy tide. We cannot put aside these realities even if we wanted to, but we can at least begin our Quaker journey in the same place, with an appreciation of the same language, the same story, the same shared history. We cannot re-enter the fervency of the early Quaker imagination, but we can appreciate it, cherish it, and hopefully add to it. Much of this acquisition concerns getting ourselves back into the habit of talking about the Quaker Way in terms of a story. Instead of the habitual British Quaker tendency of speaking purely in negatives, ('we do not have creeds, hymns, priests') we could start talking affirmatively: 'Quakers are here because nearly four centuries ago a group of seekers felt the presence of Jesus among them, and we are still trying to work out what this means for us.' Or: 'In Quakers everyone is a priest and a pastor'. Or: 'In Friends we know God powerfully within our own hearts'. This tone implies a reorientation of attitude, a shift from purely personal assertion to a broader collective affirmation of what matters to us. Instead of throwing out the past or personalising it to the point of irrelevance, we need to dig down into our collective storehouse of wisdom, and by so doing, find the impetus to walk together.

This may bring uncomfortable ghosts to the surface for some Friends who have chosen Meeting's creedless-ness as a protective shield against words like 'God', Jesus', 'sin' or 'forgiveness'. But these thorny words hold the key to why our Quakerism *is the shape it is*. Take, for instance, the Quaker vision of Testimony. As Rachel Muers reminds us, our current list of 'testimonies,' often given the acronym 'SPICE' (Simplicity, Peace, Integrity, Community) is of relatively recent date, becoming common among both British and American Quakers in the 1980s.[54] This formulation constituted a significant departure from an earlier more expansive understanding. In earlier generations testimony did not comprise particular modes of action, much less specific social stances. Rather, testimony was understood as forms of public, Spirit-led commitment that encompassed every aspect of life.[55] The latter formalisation of 'testimony' into 'the Testimonies' have gifted contemporary Friends with some definite descriptive advantages. Not only has the generality of the SPICE list allowed Friends to better explain themselves in secular non-Quaker contexts, but the Testimonies have also served as handy summaries of Quaker postures and stories for Friends themselves. As Muers notes: 'At least in some of their applications, the testimony lists *opens up* spaces for reflection, interpretation and action' in ways analogous to creedal formulae in other ecclesial traditions.[56] But the contemporary narrowing of testimony has also carried with it a particular temptation which has contributed to the general fragmentation of Liberal Quakerism. The 'list' model has encouraged Friends to treat this Quaker shorthand as something akin to an organisational statement of values, which can, to some extent, be separated from other things Quakers might do or say, including Worship and theology. In this vein, Philpott writes: 'I am Quaker ... because I have been impressed by what Quakers have done are doing. What Quakers do is intimately bound up with the values they hold – and these values are summed up in their testimonies of peace, equality, truth, and simplicity.'[57] But such an explanation misses something crucial. The things we do under the rubric of testimony are not adjuncts to our Worship or what we say about God. Rather, testimony concerns the lived outworking of what we discover as we walk the Quaker Way. They constitute the outcomes of the Quaker experiment, the fruit of our Quaker story – what we are able to do based on what we say and remember about ourselves. Put in this way, Friends are able to speak of peace, not because we simply want to be good Humanitarians, but because of the words we use and have used about God and Jesus. Similarly, Friends are able to speak cogently of Equality, not on account of justice alone, but because of the unifying Spirit we know and have known in our gathered waiting together. Likewise, integrity is a coherent posture because of our continuing trust in the Light's capacity to reveal the truth. When these verdant leaves are removed from the original Quaker tree of Worship and waiting, they are liable to curl and wither into bland statements of goodwill, rather than expressions of a holistic Quaker life.

I can already sense the twitches of acute unease among Friends who feel that what is being proposed here is nothing short of a 'return to Christian orthodoxy'. Doubtless a Friend will ask: 'To be in this shared story, do I have to believe, (as early Friends did) in the virgin birth, the Incarnation, and the possibility of miracles?' My answer is 'no', if by 'believe' we mean an abstract assent to a story that we have not lived in, or perhaps we could say, lived through, first. Sacred stories are rarely what we think they are, namely an implicit list of absolutes. As the philosopher Hannah Arendt once observed: 'Storytelling reveals meaning without committing the error of defining it.'[58] When we engage with the contours of a story, we discover that multiple interpretations may arise from the encounter, just as a fresh retelling can often reveal new truths and insights seemingly invisible at first glance. Thus, we should think of our Quaker narrative, not as tablets of stone, but as lenses through which we can see life in new ways, or as broad categories that help us organise our experience. Thus, we can define the Quaker story as that shared place from which we seek answers, containing our discoveries in the garb of practice, speech, and thought. While the big story we are cloaked in might be a challenge to summarise, (just as a fish with speech would be hard-pressed to encapsulate the ocean in which she swims), we can begin the process of articulation by being attentive to the words and symbols in our Quaker tradition. This process is not about pickling Quaker identity into any permanent configuration, but is about starting with the rich bed of resources which are implicit in the Quaker way of seeing, speaking, and relating. Think of these distinctive markers of Quaker identity as miniature maps, which induct us into a particular interpretation of the world. Living out this interpretation is more important than a series of abstract questions about God. A satisfactory vision of God is never going to come about by adopting an over-arching theory or belief. But a deep coherence may arise if we become attentive to the language and tales Quakerism uses to illustrate (perhaps we should say picture) what God is for us. This process has many dimensions, but the most crucial one it seems to me, is about recovering a sense that our words and stories come from somewhere and have the capacity to lead us somewhere else. It is about saying, 'I am a Quaker because this shared story calls to the very depth of my life – it fits the pieces of my experience together, it shapes, it heals, it clarifies.'

In this way, a return to shared story is not a call for theological purity, or conformity of belief. Liberal Friends drink from many wells, and let that liberality continue. Let us never forget that Wisdom comes from diverse quarters. What is being asked for in talk of roots is a recovery of the things that can give our individual spiritual journeys coherence. Instead of restricting us, this sense of a shared direction will aid us in deepening our love and care for one another. We may find riches within Zen practice, the call of wild nature, or the rhythms of Jewish prayer. The point is not to cast away our past (or the Wisdom which lies beyond Christianity), but to view our lives through the lens of a larger story, a core, a centre, which keeps us going when other wells run dry along the path. Speaking for myself, the shape of my spiritual biography has been deeply enriched by contemporary earth-based spiritualities, either indigenous traditions, or re-imagined constructions. Sitting on my bookshelf alongside *Quaker Faith and Practice*, one can find modern Druid, eco-theological, and Wiccan authors. Nonetheless, because I am a walker in the Quaker Way, anything that I bring from outside is not about me and 'my insights' or identity, but should exist in the service, and for the benefit, of the Quaker community. As Paul puts it in Ephesians: 'Let no unwholesome talk come out of your mouths, but only what is helpful for building up the one in need and bringing grace to those who listen' (4:29). This is the key point. Every wanderer needs a home. Let us be at home as Quakers, in the Quaker house, with all its treasures, memories, and amenities. We can bring much-needed supplies in, but only if it supports the ongoing flourishing of the whole Quaker household. We do not have the spiritual luxury of bringing food in, then labelling it (in the manner of shared student houses everywhere), 'mine'. We must therefore select and sift our insights with care, because we will be held accountable for what we choose. The question always needs to be asked: Does my spiritual walk build others up? Does it communicate grace? Or is my walk really about egoistically asserting myself? Once we turn away from the isolated self of Jones, we discover new possibilities for belonging. What does this narrative approach to Quaker life mean for our talk of God and the Spirit? In the next chapter, I argue that it is our unwillingness to embrace the specificities of a rooted Quaker story, which has led to contemporary arguments between self-identified Quaker Theists and Non-Theists. As I will seek to show, these polarities, far from representing an expression of Quaker speech, are interlopers from a secular terrain outside the Quaker household. Using the narrative template set out in this chapter, I offer a third way between these two positions, which forces us both to come to terms with distinctly Quaker conceptions and priorities.

2

Quaker Theology: Recovering the Language of Hope

The Unquiet Presence of God

Over the last two decades there has been renewed discussion among British Quakers concerning the meaning and centrality of God language in our Meetings for Worship. Do Quakers know what to say about God? Can we speak of the divine collectively? Or must we only speak for ourselves? Is God-language even needed in our life together? Some of this questioning has been clandestine, appearing as little flecks of controversy at an otherwise harmonious gathering, heard, not so much as a growl of displeasure, but as a whisper of deep discomfort. At other times, however, differences of perspective have emerged much more overtly, spilling over onto the letter pages of *The Friend,* or more locally, through a thorny piece of vocal ministry in an Area Meeting which has caused Elders to reflect on significant differences of belief and understanding between Friends. Underneath these occurrences, the same problem persists; namely, what to make of the profound divergences of theological (or, indeed, anti-theological) understanding. What do they say about our sense, or lack of it, of being a Spirit-led community? Some might interpret such variance less as a gift and more as a mark of a destabilising incoherence. As Simon Best remarked gloomily back in 2010:

> There is an argument that Quaker theology, with its emphasis on continuing revelation and change, is inherently radical. However I suggest that rather than being radical, having a theology so open that people can believe anything and still join shows that we are scared of having a tradition, and of

being faith based and spiritually grounded. By being totally open, by accepting all theologies, and even those with no theology but a philosophy, we may include people, but we also exclude others. British Quakerism has become an orthopraxy rather than an orthodoxy.... In religious groups a strong surface culture can disguise an absence of deep faith.[59]

As Best was at pains to show, the thorny matter of God has not merely illuminated deep conceptual divisions but has called into question the very notion of Quaker corporate witness. As Best notes, echoing Ben Pink Dandelion: 'Today Quakers can "choose their Gods and choose their intimacies." The de-theologisation of Quakerism is marked by individuals no longer seeing their Quaker involvement as a religious exercise.'[60] Where have these gulfs in understanding come from? While the concerns that Best expressed were hardly new, the character of the problem he addressed was much amplified by the remarkably febrile social atmosphere of the early part of the twenty-first century. While the deep-seated roots of the current controversy can doubtless be traced to the Liberal Quakerism of the mid-nineteenth century, the latest chapter in this saga of Quaker pluralism has more recent origins. Much contemporary anxiety concerning both 'God' and 'religion' within the Society can be traced to the rubble of the Twin Towers on the morning of September 11, 2001. In the aftermath of the attack, politicians, policymakers, and religious leaders became preoccupied, not merely with the problem of religion and violence, but faith's role, if any, in an increasingly secular culture. The publication of Richard Dawkins' 2006 polemic *The God Delusion*, ignited a series of fierce social debates around religious belonging, theological unreason, and Church decline. A year later, the provocative prose of Christopher Hitchens' book *God Is Not Great* added to a general atmosphere of spikey secularism, which had little patience with any appeal to divine knowledge or religious authority. Dawkins' and Hitchens' prickly rhetoric not merely insisted that religious beliefs were false, but positively wicked. Reflecting wider social concerns, particularly in the United States, the self-described New Atheist Movement spawned by such bombast, utilised its general philosophical and scientific claims to discredit both the Fundamentalist Christianity of the American Right and the ultra-traditionalist wings of both Western Islam and Judaism. In this now familiar mode of culture war, Liberal religiosity felt itself squeezed between extremes.

As the last remark intimates, British Quakers were hardly immune from this marked change in cultural climate. Indeed, many Friends imbibed it, becoming increasingly hostile to claims that Quakers needed theology, or could even be described as a 'religion'. Meetings that just a generation before had confronted a fissure between Christocentrism and Universalism, now felt the cultural conversation shift in ways that made them question received ways of talking about the spiritual life. Traditional Christian language became increasingly problematic in ways that reflected a much broader societal shift. As a consequence, matters of belief increased in urgency. This culminated in a new rift, between Friends who treated God-language as the expression of an objective and external reality, and those who regarded such language symbolically, as the expressions of all-too-human ideals. By 2014, British Quakers were agonising over the division between Quaker Theism on the one hand, and Quaker Non-Theism on the other. To some degree both labels professed to be answers to the combative tone of the New Atheism that had ignited such public discussion earlier in the century. Self-described Theists like Derek Guiton have sought to contain the spectre of Quaker Secularization through a robust return to the familiar mysticism of Rufus Jones. Treating Jones' perennial religious appeal as a Liberal Quaker minimum, Guiton has placed particular emphasis upon notions of 'transcendent' reality,[61] direct mystical experience,[62] and 'the case for God in a Quaker framework'.[63] He suggests that the reassertion of these trajectories, are the only means of giving contemporary Quakerism back its coherence. As Guiton summarises these preoccupations:

> It was faith in the reality and meaning of the 'Teacher Within' that separated the first Quakers not only from the Calvinists and other 'professors of Christianity', but from the Ranters who held pantheistic beliefs that were in the last analysis indistinguishable from materialism. It is my personal view that if Friends are to survive as a religious society, and avoid descending into a modern form of Ranterism, we will need to re-discover ourselves as a community of faith as well as experience. That faith can be broad in scope, but at the very least, it must contain some element of the transcendent, by which I mean an acknowledgement that the experience of which we speak is of something both deep within and at the same time beyond our finite human nature.[64]

Since the details of such a faith are left vague, where does this position lead Guiton regarding the nature of God? While fleeting mention is made of Incarnational theologies,[65] as the term Theism implies, Guiton wants to make general claims about the divine that could be intelligible across a range of disparate religious traditions, and more importantly, within diverse Quaker meetings. In this way, the language of mysticism has the same function for Guiton as it does for Jones, as a generic category of spiritual experience that can include varied traditions and theological claims. Using this framework as a base, Guiton imagines God as 'the source of love', a 'Mystery'[66] (in the manner of Pseudo-Dionysius the Areopagite) and Being-itself within and beyond the world we know through measurement and experience.[67] The distinctly Liberal Quaker content comes when Guiton attempts to fit this conception of God into the context of Quaker community. Like Rufus Jones, Guiton is keen to unmoor such general claims from any particular theological or confessional framework. Indeed, he suggests in typical modern Quaker fashion that when one looks at Quaker faith, one observes the outworking of a universal revelation shared by 'holy men and women of all faiths and none'.[68] While for Guiton, Jesus provides a unique example of 'a fully human personality open to the Spirit of God to such an extent that in Jesus we see God's nature revealed',[69] Guiton is wary of ascribing any straightforwardly Christian framework to his talk of God. Indeed he makes repeated efforts in published work to distance historical Quaker claims from what he calls 'orthodox Christianity'.[70] Alongside such universalism, Guiton also reprises Jones' noted appeal to interiority, reassuring the reader that early Friends 'were inclined to speak of the resurrection and transfiguration and ascension of Jesus not so much as historical facts, but as spiritual realities unfolding in the individual soul'.[71] What does such a religiosity amount to? As Guiton summarises his proposed posture:

A theology of this kind is not what we call today 'fundamentalism'. It is theistic without necessarily being Trinitarian, and therefore has the potential to unite Friends in the essentials. It provides an area of acceptable belief, being neither Christian orthodoxy with its more problematic dogmas, like the virgin birth, miracles, and the physical resurrection, nor flatline atheistic humanism, but a coherent and open theology filling the broad space between these extremes and expressing the rich vein of mystical Christianity which lay at the heart of early Quakerism.[72]

In a world of combative secularism, such a faith makes few concrete claims that would unsettle the nominally anti-religious hearer. While talk of transcendence might draw mild derision from secular observers, it is a transcendence which is generic enough to be perceived as harmless. It makes few historical claims and rarely attaches itself to particular contested persons or events. It is premised upon a feeling of 'faith' but the object of that emotion in Guiton is hardly clear. The God at the centre of such a Quakerism is universal, nebulous and without a definite story. Such a theology, while doubtless inclusive, leaves the presumptions of its Humanist neighbours relatively undisturbed. The same of course can be said of Quaker Non-Theism, which actively embraces the theological negations foreshadowed in its Theistic counterpart. If the Quaker Theist cannot stomach traditional Christian dogmas about Jesus and his Resurrection or Ascension as real or literal, Non-Theism extends such a metaphorical sentiment to other components of Quaker religious furniture, rendering pictures of God as wholly symbolic. Such a move frequently ends with the conflation of God-talk with ideal social values or so many helpful fables. Such Friends do not dispute that traditional notions of God, as 'real', 'external' or objective, have no rational or metaphysical relevance. But what they do dispute, often with great eloquence, is the continuing moral and aesthetic significance of God-language. As a symbology of human ideals, religiosity is still the most serviceable mode of communal expression. Thus the vitality of Quakerism should come, not from a sense of divine otherness, but from a well-trodden language of hope and reform, which has sprung up from this sense of otherness. But whether we choose Boulton's Blakean materialism or Guiton's Liberal mysticism, fundamental secular presuppositions about life and religion remain untouched. At first glance this seems a surprising conclusion. It may be supposed, (not least by Boulton and Guiton themselves), that it is a simple matter to consign these two interpretations of Quakerism to separate philosophical poles, one called transcendence, the other named imminence.

Indeed, if we attend to the grand statements of Quaker Theism and Non-Theism we may come to believe that we are dealing with opposites. But such a conclusion would be profoundly misleading. While both Quaker Theism and Non-Theism differ on precise details of claim and counterclaim, they exemplify a remarkable similarity at the level of philosophical priorities. They are both reticent to explore the historical specificity of Quaker God-language. They both delight in keeping their notion of religious life vague, one in an effort to make space for an acceptable God between Christianity and Humanism, the other to make space for God's Humanistic reinterpretation. Even Guiton, who wishes to give Christian legacies a more respectful hearing in the Society, is surprisingly uninvested in the particulars of the Christian story itself, beyond a general kind of 'faith'.[73] As Rhiannon Grant has vividly noted on the latter point:

> Guiton is as bound by the general Quaker tendency towards apophatic or negative theology as any of his nontheist interlocutors. It [God] must transcend people, but perhaps not the universe. It is transcendent but need not be personal; it does not have, for example, any specifically Christian characteristics. A mischievous philosopher might find grounds for arguing that Guiton is nearly a nontheist, especially if the nontheism in question is a confidently mystical rather than wholly materialist one.[74]

This unlikely convergence of perspectives draws to our attention the fact that neither Guiton nor Boulton regard Christian God-language as in any sense essential or regulative for Quaker life. Individuals may of course deploy specific pieces of Christian language in verbal ministry, but these constitute little more than a preference. The possibility left wholly uninvestigated, even in Quaker Theism, is the claim that Christian language is essential to Quakerism, and that such language actually allows us to form a sense of the God at the centre of our Worship, an Ultimate with particular qualities. This path is largely unavailable even to the Quaker Theist, since she, like the Non-Theist, is under the auspices of the Liberal 'absolute perhaps'. Here the desire to include and generalise becomes stronger than the desire to say unambiguously Quaker things about life, faith, or God. Guiton speaks for many Quaker Theists and Non-Theists alike when he insists that while early Friends lived and reflected within the confines of Christianity alone, modern Friends need not do so.[75] This fact speaks to a more general reality within the Religious Society of Friends. Centuries ago, Medieval Christendom promoted a pernicious theology of supersession. States and churches took the view, often backed by force, that Jewish communities should be pitied and despised on account of following an inferior and degenerate faith which had been supplanted by the superior light of Christianity. Today, among British Quakers, a new form of supersessionism is afoot, the often-unexamined belief that 'we' modern Quakers have rightly transcended some narrow and ill-informed creature called *Paleo-Quakerism*. There are thankfully no brutal edges to this contemporary theology of replacement, but there is a stunning trivialisation of Quaker language and memory under the guise of educated charity. The matter is commonly expressed like this. While George Fox, Mary Penington and William Penn did the best they could with a limited set of spiritual materials, we contemporary Liberal Friends now understand the full challenge and benefits of religious diversity. We understand, as our ancestors did not, that we share the planet with many old and venerable spiritual traditions. And in a globalized world, we enlightened religious liberals should be willing to throw away most elements of our Christian past to achieve greater fellowship. We are, the Liberal narrative runs, thankfully freed from the burden of a parochial and outdated story. The

Christian language of God is the first and most obvious casualty in the promulgation of this attitude. Out of this liberal soil come Friends who routinely and unthinkingly reject so-called 'biblical' notions of God in sweeping terms, an approach they would be reluctant to adopt with other traditions such as Buddhism or Islam. The same Friends often speak contemptuously of attempts to talk theologically about their experience in ways that too closely resemble the Christian tradition. As the last chapter suggested, such dismissals have the unfortunate result of cutting us off from the deep words, imagery and grammar that permeates Quakerism. It leaves us rootless and without a thicker sense of collective experience and shared history.

How then do we move beyond the vague images of God offered by Quaker Theism and Non-Theism alike? In this chapter, I offer an extended meditation upon George Fox's understanding of the story of Scripture. I argue that a robust recovery of Fox's understanding of the meaning and function of biblical witness provides the key to reviving a sense of shared Quaker God-language. In the first part of this discussion, I propose a fundamental reorientation of our common Jonesian understanding of the Light, towards Fox's holistic sense of the Light as that which connects Friends to a vast spiritual history which encompassed prophets and seekers, sinners, and saints. In Meetings gathered by the Spirit, Fox trusted that this shared story should frame, order, and make sense, not merely of Friends' Worship together, but the particulars of Friends' personal experiences. One could look into the story and see in its many figures – Moses and Pharaoh, Sarah and Hagar, Lot and Abraham, the inward state of one's own life. At the centre of this ever-living history for Fox was Jesus Christ, divine wisdom made flesh, who could speak to Friends' diverse conditions. For Fox it was He who made the words of Scripture into an immediate reality, a story intended, not merely to recount the past, but to transform the present. Thus for Fox, all true readings of Scripture were incarnational, that is, they involve the words of Scripture becoming flesh in events and deeds. Building upon this account, the second part of this chapter argues that Fox's theology opens up the possibility of a revived universal, inclusive Quakerism, rooted in the promise of a God of radical justice and fiery love. Premised in a space beyond the stale totalities of belief or non-belief, I suggest how such a vision can help us live in a dark world with hope. When individual accounts of self-creation and autonomy give out, the God of our Worship is waiting for us, ready to propel us into a larger life, fusing past and present, Heaven and Earth.

Fox's Puritan Milieu and the Light Within

When we strip away the archaic language and frequently esoteric professions of saving faith, George Fox's *Journal* is a story about stories. Fox's narrative begins with a brief mention of the personal histories that have made him. His godly father, Christopher Fox, is described 'as by profession a weaver, an honest man',[76] while his mother, Mary Lago, is recalled as issuing from the 'stock' of those Puritan martyrs who died under the religious purges of Mary Tudor.[77] Both remarks reveal something crucial about the young George's mental furniture. In the seventeenth century, there was a popular perception of weavers as particularly inclined to forms of radical Protestantism.[78] As George's description of his mother further confirms, the Foxes were not children of the Reformation in a general sense, but beneficiaries of that rich stream of theological teaching that had issued from the pen of John Calvin in Geneva. With his stern doctrine of absolute divine sovereignty and complete human depravity, Calvin had left one option open to Christians – *to believe God's promises in Scripture and surrender to the divine will in all things*. Submission was the key posture of the Geneva teaching, a stark obedience to what we are called ultimately to be, namely adopted children of God. In this endeavour, the chief lifeboat was Scripture, which for Calvin constituted the only 'spectacles' through which sinful creatures could comprehend the works and glory of God.[79] In their arrogance, the Medieval Scholastics had believed it was possible to discern the character of God from the neutral postulates of natural reason. Yet Calvin (like Luther) affirmed that there was no neutral starting place from which to understand the divine, no abstract vantage from which to know the Absolute. To attempt such a move, Calvin warned, would invariably lead to the mind's capture by entirely human notions which flatter and bolster what people already believe. As Calvin reflects at the beginning of his grand treatise *The Institutes of Christian Religion*:

> Those, therefore, who, in considering this question, propose to inquire what the essence of God is, only delude us with frigid speculations, it being much more our interest to know what kind of being God is, and what things are agreeable to his nature. For, of what use is it to join Epicures in acknowledging some God who has cast off the care of the world, and only delights himself in ease? What avails it, in short, to know a God with whom we have nothing to do?[80]

Such minds, says Calvin, '[instead] of ascending higher than themselves as they ought to do, they measure him (God) by their own carnal stupidity, and, neglecting solid inquiry, fly off to indulge their curiosity in vain speculation.'[81] Instead of wallowing in these manufactured images of God, Calvin bids his reader to speak of the divine from the context of a gathered religious story and a concrete community of faith, from which we can learn of God's true nature and attributes. Christian narrative is the key to such knowledge believes Calvin, since its doctrine is rooted, not in upholding human knowledge, but in stripping the self of its pretentions to certainty and understanding. In the ruins of our humbled minds, thought

Calvin, true comprehension of the Godhead could spring forth, if properly instructed. This approach to the spiritual life illuminates a second key posture beloved of the Puritan; that of trust. If we clutched to what Scripture revealed, our lives could be filled with the assurance that despite ourselves, God would accomplish his providential power in us. But for the Puritan, there was no trust without anxiety, no hearing God's promises without a fierce examination of them, as they pertained to one's own life. Such a creed was often fraught with apprehension, terror, and tears. Hell was a real prospect, and since God had already decided upon the collection of the saved before the beginning of the world (Rev. 13:8), the possibility of predestined perdition always lurked at the edge of Puritan consciousness. Yet, the fires of damnation were counterbalanced by Calvin's lavish insistence upon the overflowing grace of God. Puritan logic ran thus: if we believe in the promises in God's story, (in salvation, the conquest of death and hell) we are freed from a sense of sin and guilt. But as Calvin insisted, even the act of faith was not dependent upon our feeble wills. The God who promised our salvation also gave us the capacity to believe in what had been promised.[82] If all is in God's hands, we can neither add to God's action through our virtue nor detract from it with our vice. Whether we feel we have morally succeeded in life or no, we are all miserable reprobates before the Throne of the Almighty. There was thus an exhilarating air of equality in the Puritan creed. In mutual sinfulness and the universal need for bountiful mercy, one discerns a paradoxical elevation of the fragile individual in Calvin's conception of the religious life. Under the dark cloud of depravity, there were no 'high' or 'low' in God's Kingdom. Thus, in temperament many Puritans were minded towards an independent congregationalism which was entirely separate from the authority either of kings or magistrates. God alone could sustain his Church and make the sick people therein well. For the Puritans, secular power had no business intruding on the work of divine healing.[83] This democratic habit of the heart would later flower in Fox's Church polity beyond the doors of the steeple house, but its theological germ was already in his childhood. But if this Puritan milieu supplied many of Fox's later preoccupations, it also seeded discontents which would later burst forth as a profound spiritual crisis. While Calvin insisted that no work of goodness could ever satisfy God, he assumed that trust in God's promises would generate a new inner life which would be radically different from an unbelieving self. As Calvin observed:

[By] faith we receive the incorruptible seed (1 Peter 1:23), by which we are born again to a new and divine life. And yet faith itself is a work of the Holy Spirit, who dwells in none but the children of God. So then, in various respects, faith is a part of our regeneration, and an entrance into the kingdom of God, that he may reckon us among his children. The illumination of our minds by the Holy Spirit belongs to our renewal, and thus faith flows from regeneration as from its source; but since it is by the same faith that we receive Christ, who sanctifies us by his Spirit, on that account it is said to be the beginning of our adoption.[84]

Understood in the terms of modern narrative theology, we might say that for Calvin, those who believe the story of Scripture enter it, that is, they become qualitatively different from people without the story. Such narrative-shaped people didn't stop being sinners in the eyes of God, but they were no longer under judgement on account of their sinfulness. Christ had brought them everlasting reprieve, despite their hateful and recalcitrant natures. Such people lived with a new sense of assurance which would in time manifest in new moral fruit, in love, patience, sobriety. Their lives were now narratively shaped by the Word of God through the aid of the Spirit, transforming them at the last, into mirrors or replicators of the Word. But this presented Fox with a problem not uncommon among the religious minds of his age. How was it that there were so many people who spoke of God's promises and said they believed, and yet their lives remained unaffected by the Word? This is the first great existential quandary of the *Journal*. Early on in the account, we see Fox interrogating the spiritual authorities around him for an answer to the relative religious flatness of people's lives to no avail. As Fox agonises over this contradiction:

> I went to another ancient priest at Mancetter, in Warwickshire, and reasoned with him about the ground of despair and temptations; but he was ignorant of my condition; he bade me take tobacco and sing psalms. Tobacco was a thing I did not love and psalms I was not in a state to sing... I saw they were all miserable comforters; and this brought my troubles more upon me. Then I heard of a priest living about Tamworth, who was accounted an experienced man, and I went seven miles to him; but I found him but like an empty hollow cask.[85]

There is something in these protestations of the disaffected Holden Caulfield in JD Salinger's *Catcher in the Rye*. Like Holden, Fox is seemingly surrounded by 'phonies' who refuse to tell the truth about themselves. They used high-flown language, but they did not know anything of what they spoke. In modern parlance, we might say that Fox's gripe was with the systematisation of Christian faith, to the neglect of prayer and the experience of Christ working in the heart. A common reply from Fox's Calvinist elders to the contradiction between essence and appearance was to insist that unchanged lives signified that such people did not have true faith by grace, only the form of it. But since nothing we could do could improve on what God had already done in securing our salvation, how could we tell the difference between true and false faith? Could Fox be certain of his own trust in the promises of Scripture? Or was his belief as shallow as the unregenerated people he met? In other words, could Fox believe in the truthfulness of his belief? These questions were tinged by the Protestant psychology of Fox's age, particularly the intense focus upon personal salvation. But Fox's concerns encompassed more than the wellbeing of his soul. This young Puritan wanted to know *what being a Christian really meant*. In this way, Fox was not on a private journey towards some free-floating authenticity, but on a quest for a true community of believers. Behind this goal lay several urgent questions: How should Fox make the contours of the biblical story live in him? How could words about God become what preachers said they were – the very Word of God? It is evident from the *Journal* that as a young man Fox attempted to solve these quandaries by searching the Bible for some proof text that would tell him how to proceed. Thus in one striking passage Fox tells us:

> [M]y relatives were much troubled that I would not go with them to the "church" to hear the priest; instead I went into the orchard or the fields, with my bible, by myself. I asked them, did not John say to believers, 'that they needed no man to teach them, but as the anointing teaches them' (1 John 2:27). Though they knew this scripture to be true, they were still upset and fearful because I could not yield to their wishes in this matter and go to hear the priest with them... So I could not join in with them or any of the dissenting groups; but I was as a stranger to all and relied entirely upon the Lord Jesus Christ.[86]

Instead of submitting to preachers and sects, Fox attempted to use the Puritan posture of submission to quell his own troubles. Fox desired not *an account* of God, but a living principle that made such accounts real and active. It was midst this profound despair of never finding such deep spiritual waters that he discovered the Light in himself. Today, Liberal Friends tend to think of the Light as synonymous with their own spiritual intuition. A century of comparative mysticism has further complicated matters among Friends by encouraging us to think of the Light as a general spark of divinity inside us, or even as a more sublime version of our daily conscience. Both these formulations make the Light seem akin to some personal, psychological capacity, which, though shared, is structured by our individual biographies and cultures. We have in part been encouraged to individualise the Light in this way because of the way Fox talks about it. He tells us, for instance, that he knew of the Light before he looked for it in the Bible. This has implied for many Quaker moderns that the Light precedes any and all religious stories, and indeed can be tailored to suit other sacred frameworks. As the Quaker Universalist Jim Pym has articulated the latter interpretation:

> There are many people of other faiths who similarly wait in silence – either in groups or on their own – to discover this Principle or Divine Essence as a living force in their lives. So it is not only a *Quaker Principle*. Christians call it "the Mind that was in Christ Jesus", or "Cosmic Christ". In Buddhism it is "The Unborn Buddha Mind" or our "Original Face". In Hinduism, it is *the Atman,* in the sense of the Self which is One with God. In China, it was known as the Tao, while the other monotheistic religions speak of "the Soul" or "the Spirit" or use phrases similar to the Quaker term, "That of God".[87]

Pym is of course right about the Light's trans-cultural quality, and in particular the distinctly Quaker willingness to see in the faiths of others a reflection of cardinal Quaker experiences. But despite the vivid beauty of the above formulation, it ignores something crucial about Fox's original experience. When Fox stumbles upon the Light, it calls him not to a general mode of religiosity, but to the God of Abraham, Isaac, Moses, and Jesus. It said: *Turn to the Scriptures and you will find a record of what you first felt within.* As Fox expressed it:

> For I saw in that Light and Spirit, which was before Scripture was given forth, and which led the holy men of God to give them forth, that all must come to that Spirit, if they would know God or Christ or the Scriptures aright, which they that gave them forth were led and taught by.[88]

The Light was revealed to Fox as that same Spirit that inspired the Prophets of Israel and empowered the Apostles. God was not a shadowy universal force, but an Absolute with a history, with a people, with a character and with an intent. In this way Fox was able to walk someway with the Calvinist world that had produced him. What Calvin had attempted to reason out through apologetics, Fox had verified through direct experience. The biblical text was a portal into this Reality, a window through which one could see the deep structure of the world. Today, many will find such emphatic religious conviction hard to understand. How can one man, sitting in one little corner of the world be so certain of the story he was born into? That in some way, the words he uses for God penetrates the very depths of existence. Why shouldn't he have done? After all, truth is always revealed somewhere. It is always disclosed to someone. Even the scientific endeavour, with its commitments to objectivity and universal testability, has a history. The truths of material and biological science were uncovered in a time and place, coloured by the circumstances of their observers. They are no less true for all that. It is doubtless contemporary prejudice that prevents us from seeing universal claims at the heart of a particular story, but this is precisely what Fox discovered as he stood in the Light.

But one should not suppose that all Fox's revelation amounted to, was a simple recognition of his faith's rightness. The God he discovered in his heart seemed profoundly alien, more alien even than the awesome divine judge of Calvin. Despite the terror and tears of his childhood faith, the Puritan Deity, its promises, and its punishments, could often be compartmentalised into an afterlife. While Puritans looked for evidence of God's work in their lives, attention would frequently turn away from the contradictions of the moment, and towards the prospect of heavenly completion. There was, thus, woven into the Puritan spirit of submission, a certain passivity towards the world and its problems. The sternness of Puritan faith could certainly produce street preacher activists, horrified by the depravity around them. But the same impulse of disgust could just as easily generate sublime fatalists for whom 'thy will be done' meant a decisive lack of human agency in any but the smallest matters. The content of Calvinist theology largely confirmed such apathy in the assertion that sin and death would be defeated, but never in this life. Injustice, personal inequity, and hardness of heart could be shrugged off under the cloak of the overflowing grace of God in a future Heaven. Fox's experience wrenched him violently away from such otherworldly expectation. The God he felt in him was not far away, passively waiting to shepherd souls into their post-mortem state. Rather, Fox sensed God as an unbounded and unruly presence, which suffused the pains and joys of ordinary life. The promise of salvation, Fox discerned, could be experienced before death. The Light of Heaven could shine, even midst the thick clouds of earth. In the glare of the Light no complete depravity of the human spirit could stand because God desired the world to be brought into the keeping of the divine embrace. And what God desired, knew Fox, God could achieve. Scripture was a testament, not to a general divinity, but to a dynamic bottomless sea of Being that wished to preserve its creatures from loss, separation, and darkness. Salvation was not an abstract matter of doctrine for Fox, but something that could sink down into our marrow. Fox's faith of radical imminence may be said to resemble in broad outline the Tolstoian Christianity of immediate experience advocated by the twentieth-century philosopher Ludwig Wittgenstein. As Wittgenstein vividly noted in a fragment from 1937:

> Christianity is not a doctrine, not I mean a theory about what has happened and what will happen to the human soul but a description of something that actually takes place in human life. For 'consciousness of sin' is a real event and so are despair and salvation through faith. Those who speak of such things, (Bunyan, for instance) is simply describing what has happened to them, whatever gloss anyone may want to put on it. (1937:28c)[89]

Thus for Fox, like Wittgenstein, faith possessed a deep closeness and sensuality that Guiton's mystical talk of a transcendent God at work in the soul doesn't quite capture. For early Friends, Salvation happened in bodies, in real times and places. Christianity was not merely concerned with a New Jerusalem coming from the clouds, but the breaking in of a muddy, messy God. In the intensity of early Quaker Meetings, Friends could often sense the divine love they spoke of, taste it, feel it, swim in it. This is the existential nucleus from which our Quaker life was first cultivated, and it is, if we desire it, a source of vitality going into the future. It was through an open-handed trust in such boundless Being that Friends discovered who they were, and how they were meant to live. The divine call, felt repeatedly by early Friends, was one which echoed throughout the Scriptures: 'Do not be afraid' (Luke 1:30). In the tender embrace of the Light, life was no theatre of accidents nor the product of impersonal fate. The creation was sustained by love, mysterious and wonderful. What should contemporary Liberal Friends make of such a vision? In the proceeding discussion, I argue that the God of Fox is both profoundly weird and yet strangely familiar. The Light that bursts forth from the Bible introduces us to a bizarre world of miracles, sages, and angels, but it also insists that what it describes is not found in some far-off place. The wonderous happenings of Scripture refer to immediate, but often untapped dimensions of our ordinary world. We can experience this *world within the world* at any moment if we are just attentive to our inner depths. Such a theology not merely refutes many of our inherent religious assumptions about a distant dualistic Godhead, but it also draws us into a refreshing and life-giving account of faith.

The God We Forgot: The Word Becoming Flesh

The first sign that something had changed in the young Puritan was a profound sense of hope. The long night was over. Words seemed to pour from Fox's mouth, burbling like clear water, shining like new glass. In the early part of the *Journal*, Fox appears as an estranged, lonely man on the very edge of his world. After the visionary experiences of 1647, Fox senses himself loved by a ceaseless power which will not let him go. But this was not merely a fleeting spiritual 'high', but constituted a fundamental reorientation of Fox's world. This new focus took the familiar words of an English Puritan's faith and drew them beyond the bounds of Christendom, both Catholic and Protestant. This radical new beginning manifested first in Fox's attitude to sin. In Fox's age, both Catholics and Puritans agreed upon the indelible stain of original sin. On this side of the grave no Christian could escape Adam's inequity. Only by grace on the threshold of heaven would the damage of sin finally be removed. But after his experience of absolute affirmation, Fox looked upon this doctrine as little more than a counsel of despair that tried to excuse human failure, while secretly questioning the transforming power of God in this world. In an epistle of

1668 Fox puts the charge thus:

> They that have lost the true hope, which purifies as he is
> pure, they have set a purgatory to cleanse them when they
> are dead. And others cry up a body of sin and death on this
> side of the grave, with their hypocrite's hope; and they have
> lost the true ministry, and set up a false one, to preach up
> imperfection. And people were imperfect in old Adam before
> Christ came; for the law made nothing perfect; but the true
> minister of Christ, the hope of glory doth make you perfect,
> both in the apostles' days and now.[90]

God at work then and now, this was Fox's central message. If
Christ had come into the world to forgive sins and besiege the
demons, that was his mission still. As the Gospels affirmed
again and again, the Spirit of Christ did not leave people as
they were but brought them into new life in the present. Christ
did not ask those in need to wait for death to be released from
their manifold personal torments. He held them in his love and
proclaimed: 'Your sins are forgiven' (Luke 7:48). Even when
Jesus faced death, his focus remained resolutely on the now. As
Jesus says to the criminal beside him on the Cross: 'Truly I tell
you, today you will be with me in paradise' (Luke 23:43). Not
after Judgement, not after a purgatorial struggle, not after Christ
reigns again, but *today*. All time was God's, but divine power
was always manifest in the stream of the present. If the Light
signified the continuing presence of Christ in the heart, then those
who worshipped in the Light could vanquish sin in themselves,
living virtuously like Zachariah and Elizabeth, 'righteous in the
sight of God, observing all the Lord's commands and decrees
blamelessly' (Luke 1:6). In place of ethereal transcendence, the
God of Fox personifies the kind of life-giving imminence that is
so characteristic of contemporary Non-Theist Quakerism. In the
light of Fox's religious vision, Jesus of Nazareth becomes the

invisible flesh of the world, imbibing those who seek him with a new moral vitality and the inner strength to be made anew. This is what is meant by an incarnational theology. Fox does not wait meekly for a distant forever, but fully expects God to be directly present to those that love and cherish the Light in themselves. This is religious humanism of a kind, but it is premised, not upon making divine depths human, but by divinizing the human world. Such a radical trajectory has the capacity to speak to many Friends today, particularly those who have been spiritual refugees from other Christian communities where the doctrine of sin was used purely as a weapon of compliance, or as an instrument of shame. In our Quaker Way, Heaven is not a future holiday for good behaviour, but an expression of what we are meant to be, beloved creatures capable of manifesting God's grace in the world. Fox teaches us that we are not cursed reprobates but candles that have simply lost our light. If we return to our original flame, allow ourselves to be ignited by the fire of divine love we will return to that house we never really left. This is the deep truth behind Fox's inquisitions at Ulverston Church in 1652: 'You will say, Christ saith this, and the apostles say this; but what canst thou say? Art thou a child of Light and hast walked in the Light, and what thou speakest is it inwardly from God?'[91]

Taken together, these questions affirm a profoundly optimistic relation between the divine and human worlds. In Fox's theology, we are not hopeless degenerates in the hands of a heavenly puppet master, but sons and daughters of a grand inheritance which will never be lost. It is ours already if only we claim it. At the heart of Fox's experiential teaching was thus a striking claim about the nature of existence. In essence, when Christians speak of 'sin' they are gesturing at the heavy chains of the past, those systems of thought and power that prevent us from renewing the forces of life under the auspices of divine love. In the wake of these immovable solidities comes brokenness, idolatry, violence, sorrow, and shame. In the widening gulf between *what should be* and *what is*, the world seems hopelessly torn. But Fox has a defiant answer to such an existential schism. Jesus Christ, the one who showed us God's Kingdom in history, will not let us be prisoners of the past. His Gospel of forgiveness is rooted in repeated cancellations of our material, historical and moral debts. His freedom is ours, and it is always present. As Jesus declares 'the kingdom of God is in your midst' (Luke 17:21). Such was the power of this vision for Fox, that he often stepped close to the claim that all who obeyed the Light became not merely true disciples of Jesus, but new manifestations of Christ on earth. In such a move the words of Scripture become energetic solidities able to match the seemingly immovable hardness of sin. Lives and bodies become centres of that power that lifted up the prophets and consoled the Apostles. Time and text mingled to create a counterforce to a world estranged.

If Fox's vision of the Gospel involved the re-spiritualisation of ordinary believers, what did this mean for notions of Church? Something of the grandeur of Fox's conception can be glanced in his creation vision of 1647. As Fox writes: '[The] creation was opened to me; and it was showed me how all things had their names given them according to their nature and virtue and that the admirable works of the creation, and the virtues thereof, may be known, through the openings of that divine Word of wisdom and power by which they were made.'[92] But enfolded in this account of divine sovereignty was, Fox saw, a task. Fox tells us in the *Journal* that 'I was at a stand in my mind whether I should practise physic for the good of mankind, seeing that the nature and virtue of the creatures were so opened to me by the Lord'.[93] The admission is interesting, not least because it reveals what Fox thought his vision must have meant. It implied a new, or perhaps we should say neglected, orientation in the lives of Christians together. Christians, like their Master, must be active agents of healing, not merely within the Church, but everywhere. In many respects, this potentially cosmic, activist model of Church represented a departure from the Puritan religion of the Word on which Fox was raised. In his Calvinist childhood, the Church was often imagined in terms of the invisible righteous remnant that stood against the many false churches of Christendom. The implication was that the Christian community should conceive of itself as an isolated cell, mindful of its purity and relentlessly focused upon maintaining its correct preaching of the Gospel. In these moves, wider questions of society and world could be deemphasised. In the preface to *The Institutes*, Calvin had expressed this stance through his refusal to identify the Church either with particular institutional forms or the conventions of worldly power. A formless Church, resting purely on the preaching of the Word of God, was the only safe road to true religion. As Calvin summarised his highly sectarian ecclesiology:

The hinges on which the controversy turns are these: first, in their contending that the form of the Church is always visible and apparent; and, secondly, in their placing this form in the see of the Church of Rome and its hierarchy. We, on the contrary, maintain, both that the Church may exist without any apparent form, and, moreover, that the form is not ascertained by that external splendour which they foolishly admire, but by a very different mark, namely, by the pure preaching of the word of God, and the due administration of the sacraments. They make an outcry whenever the Church cannot be pointed to with the finger. But how oft was it the fate of the Church among the Jews to be so defaced that no comeliness appeared? What do we suppose to have been the splendid form when Elijah complained that he was left alone? (1 Kings xix. 14). How long after the advent of Christ did it lie hid without form? How often since has it been so oppressed by wars, seditions, and heresies, that it was nowhere seen in splendour? Had they lived at that time, would they have believed there was any Church? But Elijah learned that there remained seven thousand men who had not bowed the knee to Baal; nor ought we to doubt that Christ has always reigned on earth ever since he ascended to heaven?[94]

In accord with such an account, the psychology of English Puritanism in the 1640s and '50s tended towards postures of insularity and endurance, an outlook that shifted attention away from the general social and cosmic promises of Scripture and towards immediate matters of ecclesial discipline and proper decorum.[95] This is not to say that Puritans were reluctant to see the Church as socially active or a transformative expression of a new creation, only that such newness was tightly hedged in and defined, to protect it from the world's corruption.[96] For Fox these old habits of mind died hard. Indeed, one could argue he never quite grew out of them. When Fox addressed early Quaker communities experiencing sporadic persecution, he repurposed this language of a righteous minority midst corruption. He felt acutely that Friends, without the forms and rites of other confessions, personified precisely the pure and essential Church that minds such as Calvin had beckoned at, but had not themselves achieved. Was Quakerism then merely Puritanism on steroids? No. Fox's visionary experiences of 1647 had changed him, forcing him beyond the habitual interpretations of Calvinist Christianity. While clutching tightly to that blessed hope of the Puritan, the genuine existence of a Church standing against the vain fashions of the world, his tender visitations had convinced him of the pressing and absolute reality of Paul's words in Romans 8:

We know that the whole creation has been groaning as in the pains of childbirth right up to the present time. Not only so, but we ourselves, who have the first fruits of the Spirit, groan inwardly as we wait eagerly for our adoption to sonship, the redemption of our bodies. For in this hope we were saved. But hope that is seen is no hope at all. Who hopes for what they already have? But if we hope for what we do not yet have, we wait for it patiently. (NIV Romans 8: 22–25)

In this vision, not only Christian believers, but the whole of creation, is predestined to be filled with the unifying Light of Christ. The Church is not merely the home of a beleaguered minority, but the active herald of a new creation that cannot be defined by sects, congregations, and buildings. At the level of individuals, this frequently manifested as a radical healing ministry rooted in prayer. As both the *Journal* and *Fox's Book of Miracles* attest, early Friends fully expected a return of the miraculous healing credited to the Apostles, and at various times they witnessed moments of miraculous cure.[97] But these examples of God's microcosmic activity merely set the stage for what Friends regarded as a greater set of tasks. At the level of human society, such a restorative *ecclesia* meant the reconciliation of a broken human family under the auspices of the Messianic promise of peace. Under the banner of 'the Lamb's War', the first Quakers confronted poverty, squalor, hatred, and despair. In a world divided by wealth, nation, and faith, Friends sought a reiteration of that venerable covenant between God and all humanity (Genesis 9:1–17). In this spirit of reconciliation, Fox is able to say 'Christ hath enlightened every man that comes into the world, he hath enlightened the Turks, Jews, and Moors, with the light, (which is the life in him the word) that all the light might know God and Christ'.[98] Towards the non-human world, Friends were to reject greed, grasping, and avoidable cruelty towards other creatures. Such was the vitality of this creation theology among early Friends, that contemporary Quaker scholarship has often spoken in terms of an early Quaker eco-theology.[99] In these interlocking models of Christian life, encompassing self, society and nature, the Second Coming was not some distant event after our deaths, but the moment when our individual lives touch that true healing and peace which is the ground of our being. This was the guiding hope of early Friends, providing the deep structure of their speech and acts. They desired to see God manifest in all they knew and loved. Can we as contemporary Liberal Friends learn from this vision? In the final part of this chapter, I consider how hope is often the missing ingredient of an increasingly elastic and fragmented British Quakerism. I argue that if we wish to recapture a substantial sense of shared hope, we will need to find ways of appreciating and transmitting a compelling reading of our distinctive Quaker narrative.

Quakerism and the Necessity of Hope

Where has this recollection of our Quaker God-talk brought us? It is perhaps a mark of our extreme secularity that many Friends, (including the present writer) frequently think about *the problem of God* in our Meetings, through resolutely sociological lenses. We ask what Theism or Non-Theism means for the future of the Society. We agonise over what such differences mean for being a loving community together. We might feel pushed, having failed to answer these issues satisfactorily, to ask that ominous query: What is 'the point' of Quakers? These questions may be valuable in their own way, but they sidestep a more profound issue. Scripture invites us to 'Always be prepared to give an answer to everyone who asks you to give the reason for the hope that you have' (1 Peter 3:15). Here, we find revealed something which is so often absent from our recent controversies regarding theology. For the writer of 1 Peter, God is not merely a hypothesis, a mere theory or belief, but an orientation towards life, an affirmation of a future in which we and the world will always be included. *Hope implies life.* To put words around our hope is to say what kind of life we feel able to live. Our God-language is a testament to a strange security that allows us to take the next step, even when the world seems dark and forbidding. As Wittgenstein once put it: 'The way you use the word "God" does not show whom you mean, but what you mean' (1946:50e).[100] In this formula, the 'what' is not just an abstract experience of something profound, it is something concrete, a definite manner of life, a Way to talk and walk. If we follow in this helpful trail, then we cannot regard the God at the centre of our Worship merely as a personal theory, proposition, or intellectual exercise. God is more than a private object held or thrown out within the confines of an enclosed biography. God-speech invites serious consideration of the kind of world we think we inhabit, and where we sense it is all going. As the theologian Stanley Hauerwas summarises this perspective:

> I believe what I write, or rather by writing, I learn what I believe. But then I do not put much stock in "believing in God." The grammar of "belief" invites a far too rationalistic account of what it means to be a Christian. "Belief" implies propositions about which you get to make up your mind before you know the work they are meant to do. Does that mean I do not believe in God? Of course not. But I am much more interested in what a declaration of belief entails about how I live my life.[101]

Quakers have a hallowed phrase for this view of the religious life, namely 'let your life preach'. This is what abstract talk of Theism or Non-Theism misses. Theological or indeed anti-theological propositions can only be tested by living them. Talk of God is a starting point for action, for love, for the ongoing reinterpretation of our lives in the context of a Life and Power beyond ourselves. A shared story is the map and frame for this process. It is a strong anchor which links our present selves with past wisdom. But if our God-speech becomes private, or maybe even wholly absent, where then comes our sense of hope that still suffuses our distinctly Quaker words? What or who now can 'speak to our condition'? Put more bluntly still, can our highly plural Liberal Quakerism ever hope for anything, particularly under the heavy embargo of the 'absolute perhaps'? Even if we found such a shared hope (unlikely though that seems), could we give a reason for our confidence? As Beth Allen recalls in the 2017 book *God, Words and Us*:

I recall a Quaker event, a discussion between a God-language Quaker and a nontheist Quaker. The presentations were carefully reasoned. We had advertised the event to other churches, and significant points were made in the discussion by two clergymen. One said that when he prepares couples for marriage, he quite often finds that the experience of loving someone else, putting someone else's interests and needs and wishes before their own, often for the first time in their lives, opened up for a couple an understanding of the love of God. The other priest asked: "I work with many people who are in the depths of misery. How do Quakers show people who are in despair, that there can be hope?" There was silence. As the chair, I asked all there "Do Friends have anything to say about this? Does anyone?" At length a nonfriend who is a professional counsellor rose and replied from her clinical experience. We Quakers had nothing to say about hope. I realised later that the two clergy has spoken from pastoral experience, and that though Friends can be deeply pastoral, we don't frame our thinking about profound healing and caring for each other in religious terms; we are more comfortable with secular language about inner growth. In focussing on intellectual thinking about God, what essential elements of religious vocabulary have we lost?[102]

Part of the answer to Allen's final question is that we have lost a definite sense of what our Quaker words about God can do for us. Many no longer trust, even if they felt comfortable with the details of the story, that this dusty narrative could progress or unblock anything in their lives. Our Quaker story has become something of an artefact in a museum, occasionally marvelled at, but always placed safely behind glass. How do we make the hope embedded in our Quaker tale a living force again? There is no instant recipe for theological revival, even if it were generally thought desirable. But perhaps one fruitful starting-point would be to strengthen our teaching ministry within the Society, and by so doing, reignite the habit of exploring our God-language together. Here teaching should not imply agreed answers but reasserting a set of Quaker coordinates that allow us to speak confidently about our way of Worship, our book of discipline, and our Quaker past. Another indispensable, if thorny dimension of such a recovery, might involve re-embedding our language of God and the Light within the contours of the biblical narrative. This doesn't mean producing some grand Bible-based catechism everyone in a Meeting must recite. Rather, it means giving each other the resources and space to refamiliarize ourselves with a text, which has, in the lives of some, caused untold hurt, hate and distrust. Confronted with the religious authorities of his own time, Jesus bemoaned those who professed knowledge of God, but denied such knowledge to others: 'Woe to you, teachers of the law and Pharisees, you hypocrites! You shut the door of the kingdom of heaven in people's faces. You yourselves do not enter, nor will you let those enter who are trying to' (NIV Matthew 23:13). Many have felt the heavy clang of the church door closed in their face. For those who have been scarred by the fundamentalism or biblicism of other traditions, our Meetings should be a space where Scripture is given new life. Let us open the Bible afresh, unshackled from the Christianities of self-hatred, bigotry, or shame. Let's trust our Inward Teacher to point us in the right direction, to make the text speak in ways that will build up, heal, and inspire. For some in our Meetings, a reassertion of Quaker narrative would mean examining Scripture for the first time. Such Friends would need guidance, tenderness, inspiration, and plenty of mirth. In this, Elders can play an indispensable role, in facilitating a generous atmosphere of discussion, study, and prayer.

But there is a much more challenging attitude which must underlie any attempt at reviving and strengthening our teaching ministry, and that is fostering a renewed trust in the particulars of our Quaker Way. There are many Friends who will be bewildered by my turn to Fox's theology and my insistence that contemporary Liberal Quakers could learn from the past. What, they might ask, do we modern Friends have to learn from a charismatic seventeenth-century preacher who believed in demons, witches, and faith healing? Here, we can discern the unmistakable tone of the early twentieth-century theologian Rudolf Bultmann, who observed: 'We cannot use electric lights and radios and, in the event of illness, avail ourselves of modern medical and clinical means and at the same time believe in the spirit and wonder world of the New Testament.'[103] We can answer such a modernist this way. Firstly, we should insist that merely *demythologising* our faith, so it does not offend the present preoccupations of secular reason, is a high road to nowhere in particular. Such a hedging in and jettisoning of our Quaker-speech is indeed an admission that our way of life is merely an artifact, a mere fig-leaf for a generalised humanism which needs no particularly Quaker foundations to stand on. Fox may have been strange, superstitious, even bigoted, but he knew what he waited for. He possessed a life and a speech suffused with hope. Can the same thing be said for we jaded moderns with our sophisticated scientific instruments, and sense of metaphysical complacency? Instead of starting where we already are, why not take the risk of jumping into something strange, unbelievable, unfamiliar, *and ours*? We should playfully tug at the openness of the professed Quaker Humanist. Are they open to the Quaker story changing them? Equally, is the Quaker Theist able to dive into the aspects of the Christian story that make some uncomfortable? Will they hide forever from the Resurrection? Or are they willing to wrestle with the wisdom and power the empty tomb may contain? Some years ago, I recall a Local Quaker Meeting adopting the slogan 'Come to Quakers and have your answers questioned'. This is precisely what the recovery of a shared story intends. But alongside the recommendation to spiritual adventure is a second possible reply to one such as Bultmann. The proposition that modernity has all the answers to which tradition must at all times submit, betrays an overinvestment in an isolated and assertive self, that is constantly trying to understand everything in a way which accords with its immediate likes and dislikes, beliefs, and prejudices. But is that all liberal religious community has become? A network for the fickle or likeminded? If so, what a despairing vision we have been led to by our liberalism. We have walked so freely that we have ended up in the middle of nowhere. If we wish to stop wandering in this labyrinthine aimlessness, we need to ask some tough questions of ourselves: Are we willing to concede that we are not the sole creators of our own life? Are we willing to concede that ours is not the only story that matters? This approach might at first feel deeply alien, even intolerant, to Friends who are used to the generality of Liberal orthopraxy. A story-led mode of religious life can be uncomfortable for natural pluralists, not least because it encourages us to say definite things about life and God. Liberal Quakers are not in the habit of being so emphatic in terms of the 'we'. We are much more comfortable, as Allen suggests with 'personal growth' or '*our* spiritual journey'. But more importantly than its concreteness, such a narrative-approach pushes us to concede that our hope is grounded not merely in brief personal consolation, but upon what we are able to say together as a story-shaped community.

Applied to the prickly subject of God, our personal experience is treated, not as a free-floating element, but something which is incorporated into the words and prayer of generations of Quakers. To this suggestion, many Quaker Theists and Non-Theists alike might fret that this renewed focus on narrative is nothing short of a creedal statement by the backdoor. Does the affirmation of a shared Quaker story mean we need to swallow all the weird and wonderful bits of the tale hook, line and sinker? No. We are not a community of biblical literalists or book worshippers. We affirm the continual illumination of God in our Meetings. Thus understanding our story and living it out, is an ongoing process of learning and appreciation. One does not wake up one morning and say 'today I happen to believe in the Resurrection of Jesus' or 'today I shall believe in Gabriel's words to Mary'. The stories of our tradition only become part of us through prayer, meditation and by lovingly applying them to our own lives, in words and deeds. In making sense of our story, we should employ two Scriptural criteria for the task. First: 'By their fruit you will recognize them' (Matthew 7:16). Be attentive to the ways fragments of the Quaker story impact and take root in your life. What happens in you and the world around you once you take the stories of Quakerism seriously? What happens when you begin to interpret your experiences in terms provided by the story? In ordering what we find, the Apostle Paul's words are brilliantly useful: 'Test everything. Keep what is good and stay away from everything that is evil' (1 Thessalonians 5:2). But this sifting process is not a private matter. It is embedded in the very flow of a Meeting's life and ministry. If you struggle with some aspect of the Quaker story, lay it before the gathered Meeting. This is where we encounter a second essential Scriptural criterion: 'do not believe every spirit but test the spirits to see whether they are from God' (1 John 4). Friends have long agonised over the standards for genuine Spirit-led insight, but Fox gives us a clue in an epistle of 1658:

> Be still and cool in thy own mind and spirit from thy own thoughts, and then thou wilt feel the principle of God to turn thy mind to the Lord God, whereby thou wilt receive his strength and power from whence life comes, to allay all tempests, against blusterings and storms. That is it which moulds up into patience, into innocency, into soberness, into stillness, into stayedness, into quietness, up to God, with his power.[104]

Prize this deep peace, trust it, seek it out. It will lead you further into the cave of wonders which is Quakerism. But such a trek will not be without disturbances or pitfalls. Sit with the things in the Quaker narrative that trouble or mystify you. Be open to the possibility of a God who will defy your expectations. In this questing spirit, when Friends read the Bible, we shouldn't be looking for points in the story where God is answering our questions (or confirming our perceptions). We should look for those moments when God is provoking questions. It is in the questions, not merely in the passive receipt of answers, that growth, love, and joy come. This speaks to our present tendency of theorising about God. The energy of our Quaker faith shouldn't come from moments of absolute clearness (some theistic or anti-theistic system) but from those moments of ambiguity, uncertainty and hidden depth which seek to train us in a life rooted in God. Tending, investigating, and loving these moments keep faith with Jones' Liberal Quakerism (always probing, always questioning) yet grounded in the Christ-event which nurtured first-generation Friends. This means wrestling with what other Christians call 'dogmas', without succumbing to their lure of system-building. We shouldn't hide from the virgin birth or the empty tomb, but rather recognize their power to unsettle our sense of the possible, the sense that we can tie everything up as an 'ism'. These events were not loci of certainty; they were, instead, disclosures of awful ambiguity. In the course of the angelic visitation, Mary of Nazareth asks 'How will this be ... since I am a virgin?' (Luke 1:34). When another Mary (Magdalene) stands before the empty tomb she asks 'Where have you laid him?' (John 11:34). Sitting in the midst of mystery does not mean having a spiritual lobotomy. Instead, such openness means asking our questions in the context of a story. In this regard, it isn't Theism we need (much less religious humanism), but a radical openness to the sheer strangeness of life as mediated through our narratives. It was Arthur C. Clarke who said 'The only way to discover the limits of the possible is to go beyond them into the impossible.'[105] Might Friends dare to strike out anew in the hope of extending the possible? I sense that Boulton and Guiton are equally hardened against this kind of attitude, partly because they both want to retain a strong version of the 'absolute perhaps'. But there is a richer terrain beyond this Liberal Quaker prohibition. The contours of this forbidden landscape were once mapped by Wittgenstein, in his beautiful reflections on the unbelievable doctrine of the Resurrection. Contemplating the supreme strangeness of the claim that a man rose from his tomb, this most modern of philosophers falls back on the young Fox's agonised Puritan question: *Can I believe in my belief?* This was Wittgenstein's answer:

[If] I am to be REALLY saved, — what I need is certainty — not wisdom, dreams of speculation — and this certainty is faith. And faith is faith in what is needed by my heart, my soul, not my speculative intelligence. For it is my soul with its passions, as it were with its flesh and blood, that has to be saved, not my abstract mind. Perhaps we can say: Only love can believe the Resurrection. Or: It is love that believes the Resurrection. We might say: Redeeming love believes even in the Resurrection; holds fast even to the Resurrection. What combats doubt is, as it were, redemption.[106]

This confirms a truth that Quakers have known for centuries. We can sense with our heart and learn with our hands. The intellect can take us far, but not to the edge of reason. The spiritual world must be understood holistically, with flesh and blood, with a heart ready to love. Spiritual things cohere through ongoing acts of compassion and mercy that make our stories about them manifest. But what if you believe that spiritual things aren't qualitatively different from 'ordinary things'? What if you think God language is outmoded? Or there is no God you can meaningfully talk about? The Quaker answer is deceptively simple: Wait. Practise. Keep working at it. The promise of Jesus is that the repeated incarnation of our words in care and justice, will open the portals of Resurrection, prayer, and redemption to us, not by telling us 'exactly what they are', but by showing us what they are. Trust the Quaker story and what manifests in front of you. If talk of a higher world irks you or leaves you cold, centre on the fruits of the story here and now, but don't throw out the words, keep them as tokens of wisdom and intent.

In this task of sustaining a present-focus, love is a gate to deep mysteries. In learning to love, we in turn learn something of what words like 'God' or 'Spirit' actually mean. Once we have ventured a little way through this door, we discover the world is suddenly different, that we see, as it were, through difference spectacles. A world where Resurrection can happen, (or at least one where we are prepared to take it seriously), is also a place where each of us can be at home. When we look across this new land we discover to our delight, not bland uniformity, but in a manner familiar to Liberal Friends, a grand, all-embracing diversity. The God that raised Jesus delights in the prospect of absolute love and perfect community. Here inclusion and pluralism are understood as marks of a divine presence, not simply human devices to avoid conflict. We include because of the kind of God we know and sense in our silence together. In this mode, we are not spiritual consumers, merely shopping for what we want, but participants in a new reality *that wants us included.* The invitation is wonderfully expressed by the prophet Isaiah: 'Many peoples will come and say, "Come, let us go up to the mountain of the LORD, to the temple of the God of Jacob. He will teach us his ways, so that we may walk in his paths." The law will go out from Zion, the word of the LORD from Jerusalem' (Isaiah 2:3). Here unity is not about a compromise, a negotiation, or a personal preference, but part of a process of being called and taught. The Messianic promise involves us trusting that God means it; that the Eternal desires the nations summoned as one family on the basis of worship. In the context of this Promise, we Friends should open our doors to the world and its diversity, not just because we are 'nice and accepting', but because we are guided by the reality and substance of such a promise. To put it more sharply, we should be 'accepting', not because we have little in particular to say, but because we have a lot to say. We have a lot to say about the shape of the world, the human longing for equity and justice, and the unity of the human family. Yet, we should say all these things based on an economy of worship, gift, and giving, not upon an ethos of rights or autonomy. Yet, choppy waters await our Quaker Way when we cease to take notion of God's Promise of divine inclusion seriously; when we metamorphose the promise into meagre moral guidance, metaphor, or optional poetry. Here lies the insubstantial road of self-religion (one with plenty of freedom but no directing hope). Let us pray and struggle with the promise, but let's not reject it out of hand. Let's be hardy and determined like Jacob in his battle with the Angel. Let's declare with Jacob our intention: 'I will not let you go unless you bless me' (Genesis 32:26). The challenge is clear. Do we Quakers dare to accept the power of such a blessing?

3

Recovering the Slow Jesus

Jesus Then and Now

We live in a world of nearly unimaginable speed. No sooner has the present moment passed before our eyes, has it been quarantined to the grey indefinite landscape of history. Modern people are quick to acquire new beliefs and practices (much quicker than their ancestors). The contemporary mind is altogether less sentimental about discarding venerable ideals or institutions. The pace of existence means that few have the time to ponder the intricacies of the past, much less estimate their worth. We are trained from the cradle to respect all that is novel and new while showing an acute suspicion towards well-worn custom. Our often-feverish mental horizons are primed to look towards the unrealized in ways that radically undercut the significance of the now and near. The shortened lifespan of our thought world is directly correlated with the revolutionary changes in networked communications and integrated markets that we call globalisation. In this world of roads and webs, time appears to be the scarcest resource. Our media cycle roars along with such disposable rapidity that it is nearly impossible to piece together the events, personalities, and problems offered to us without a filter. We turn to a trusted news source, a political ideology, or a trustworthy social network to anchor ourselves midst the flow of events. This fact introduces us to one of the many paradoxes of the contemporary period. We live in an age of seeming democratisation of information, but our ready access to knowledge has paradoxically given rise to a new class of gatekeepers who promise, some sincerely, some disingenuously, to describe and order the endless flow of facts. Thus, more than ever before, people hanker for complete stories to make sense of their lives. The same was true in George Fox's era in the sphere of religion. In a world where a divinely appointed king could be slain, the House of Lords dissolved, and the Church purged of its former theology, what could Englishmen of the mid-seventeenth century hold onto? A plethora of priests and theologians offered their congregations complete descriptions of the manner of the End Times, the nature and work of Christ in the English Commonwealth and what they must do to be saved. All the willing congregants had to do was accept these systematic presentations whole. But Fox, risking accusations of Ranterism, argued that one could not come to an appreciation of Jesus through elaborate doctrine, but only by allowing Christ to teach each believer Himself. Immediacy and not dogmatics would be the defining feature of this strange people who would in time become proficient in both. As Francis Howgill recalled his stunning induction into the Quaker Way:

> The Lord of Heaven and earth we found to be near at hand, and, as we waited upon him in pure silence, our minds out of all things, his heavenly presence appeared in our assemblies, when there was no language, tongue nor speech from any creature. The Kingdom of Heaven did gather us and catch us all, as in a net, and his heavenly power at one time drew many hundreds to land. We came to know a place to stand in and what to wait in; and the Lord appeared daily to us, to our astonishment, amazement, and great admiration, insomuch that we often said one unto another with great joy of heart: 'What, is the Kingdom of God come to be with men? And will he take up his tabernacle among the sons of men, as he did of old? Shall we, that were reckoned as the outcasts of Israel, have this honour of glory communicated amongst us, which were but men of small parts and of little abilities, in respect of many others, as amongst men.'[107]

This passage reveals something vital about the early Quaker attitude to Jesus. While the experience of Christ often came as a sudden flash among early Friends, their approach was always to wait in the event, letting it slowly sink into them. Jesus was near, he was present, he sat among a community of uncertain waiting people. To be with Jesus was to harken to a growing seed, to nurture a grace which would steadily change the worshipper from the inside out. The gradualness of the experience is key to early Quaker phenomenology. For Howgill, as well as other early Friends, Jesus was the One who accompanies, walks beside, and encompasses. He is known in ways that mature and unfurl. Unlike the temporal scarcity of modern globalisation or the urgent frenzy of the English revolution, this Jesus gave time back its dignity. Thus, we can say that this was a decidedly *slow Jesus*. This designation can be understood in two senses. Firstly, the Quaker Jesus-experience was slow in a personalist capacity. The one who appears, and dwells is not known all at once. Like objects and people in the ordinary world, the Jesus of early Friends is known with time, through observation and increased familiarity. We must regularly visit Him if we wish to know who Jesus is. But the embryonic Quaker sense of Jesus was slow in another key respect. He was slow just in the way that a walking pace is slow. He never strayed far from those who loved him, and always made himself part of their daily lives, mindful of their present course and capabilities. For early Friends, Jesus would never vanish without leaving word, or bewilder his Church by running on ahead. Worship was an experiment in, and an expression of, a holy posture of staying put, a steady refusal to leave the task of incremental spiritual knowing. Thus, what Fox offered was not strictly a system, but rather a posture, a way of being that permitted each person to meet Jesus in terms they could grasp in their innermost selves, in their own time. Notions were devalued, while the conception of unfolding experience was immeasurably elevated.

Yet today many Liberal Friends seem to struggle with the person of Jesus precisely because he feels so hedged in with multiple notions, systems, and claims. Many of the ecclesial refugees among us find Jesus not merely baffling but at times painful. Such discomfort frequently manifests as the Jesus of a repressive childhood. This stern Saviour is frequently the repository of all our resentment against arbitrary authority, abuse, or shame. Even when such animus is wholly absent, many Friends find it difficult to understand the often-extravagant theological claims made about Jesus by other Churches. His status as Son of God and cosmic Redeemer regularly confounds and perplexes those more obviously unitarian Quakers who are otherwise affectionate towards Jesus the earthly teacher. So how do we overcome such estrangements? My objective in this chapter is not to suggest any counterclaims for those Quakers who remain bewildered or sceptical about the person of Jesus. Rather, I want to uncover *the slow Jesus* as told and envisioned through our Quaker tradition, paying particular attention to the ways that such a retelling and imagining meets the deep spiritual needs of our diverse Liberal Quaker family. In doing so, I will seek to avoid straying too far from our Quaker story or getting entangled in arguments over the literalness or historicity of theological claims. My motivation for such a roundly narrative approach is three-fold. Firstly, it emerges from an acknowledgement of the relative futility of what theologians formally call apologetics. Too much ink has been spilt over the centuries 'arguing the case for Christ' with little added to the conversation except an excessive self-righteousness or hostility. The present writer neither wishes to encourage such vices in himself nor in the reader. Instead, I seek to find ways of making our stories about Jesus' portals to wisdom, love, and liberation. Secondly, I have no desire to trespass on that venerable scholarly debate concerning *the Jesus of faith* versus *the Jesus of history*. I happen to agree with David

Boulton that seeking out some essential Jesus behind the New Testament is probably an academic highway to nowhere. The Greek Scriptures come to us as fully theological documents in which historical events are already being recorded through the lens of the early Christian community's emerging theology and worship. There is no neutral vantage point from which to divide event from theology and theology from event. As Boulton has expressed the problem, 'the only Jesus we can be sure of is the Jesus of literature.'[108] This is not to say that nothing historical underlies these interpretations of Jesus (as Boulton and I both concede), only that we cannot be certain of our facts according to conventional historical methods and standards. The Gospels as a point of genre, are not biographies. They are testimonies of communities already transformed by the living and risen Christ. They are records of a faith already being lived, not mere recollections of the past. Doubtless, to the surprise of some, the present writer is not daunted by this observation. If we cannot be certain of any historical reconstruction, then all we have is our story and how it intersects with our lives. We are freed from the dubious task of 'discovering the real Jesus' and instead are invited to discover the living Jesus that arrives in our gathered meetings, in our prayer and in our reading. In this regard, I find myself ever more sympathetic to the words of the American Quaker poet John Greenleaf Whittier who wrote in 1870:

They fail to read clearly the signs of the times who do not see that the hour is coming when, under the searching eye of philosophy and the terrible analysis of science, the letter and the outward evidence will not altogether avail us; when the surest dependence must be upon the Light of Christ within, disclosing the law and the prophets in our own souls, and confirming the truth of outward Scripture by inward experience; when smooth stones from the brook of present revelation shall prove mightier than the weapons of

Saul; when the doctrine of the Holy Spirit, as proclaimed by George Fox and lived by John Woolman, shall be recognized as the only efficient solvent of doubts raised by an age of restless inquiry.[109]

My endorsement of this sentiment should not suggest any kind of textual fundamentalism, or inward-facing spirituality on my part. To recognise the centrality of Jesus as an inward reality should not imply a sealed community that refuses to engage with the field of historical analysis. What I am attempting to express is rather a properly Quaker criterion for interpreting our talk about Jesus. Put succinctly, this principle might be stated: *we can only test the value of our stories through our stories.* Biblical criticism and the glare of history might disturb us if facts were all that concerned us. They are not. As Friends, we seek more than a reconstruction of a world which is dead and gone. Rather we hanker after a living relation with the spiritual domain Scripture records. This frees us to love the biblical narrative, not as a portal to some unvarnished past history, but as a map of the immediate terrain and character of the divine world. This focus on direct experience leads us to my third rationale for a narrative approach. I wish to underscore the ways in which the New Testament and the Jesus depicted therein, can bind us together as Quakers, even if we differ profoundly at the level of theology or metaphysics. In coming to terms with Jesus, through the stories told and retold about him, and by inviting those stories to live in us, and change us, we discover a renewed sense not merely of personal mission, but Quaker coherence. As I go on to show, the Jesus that emerges in the twenty-seven books of the Greek Scriptures has things that will comfort us and confound us regardless of the particular quadrant of the Quaker world we happen to inhabit. Whether we speak in the accent of Universalism, Theism, Non-Theism or Christocentrism, Jesus will have a message for us, one that both grounds and challenges, affirms and questions who we are and what we believe. In these pages, I hope to do justice to Jesus' many-sidedness in ways that enrich and extend our understanding of that slow Messiah our Quaker foremothers and forefathers trusted with such zealous love.

Christ-Centred Quakers: The Challenge of Pentecost

For those who call themselves Christ-centred Friends, the gifts of Jesus seem so apparent they need little exposition. The promises of Christ are understood by such Friends as *their inheritance* and *their hope*. When Jesus speaks of the Father's many mansions, such Friends often feel, with an understandable intensity, their place in the heart of God. For this species of Quaker, the life, death, and Resurrection of Christ are keenly felt, not just as abstract sacred facts, but as springs of living water, bubbling up from moments of love, gift-giving, and prayer. In the silence of Meeting, such Friends hear the consolation of Christ's farewell discourse, ringing clear as a bell: '[The] Advocate, the Holy Spirit, whom the Father will send in my name, will teach you all things and will remind you of everything I have said to you. Peace I leave with you; my peace I give you. I do not give to you as the world gives. Do not let your hearts be troubled and do not be afraid' (John 14: 26–7). But like all oases of calm, an acute temptation is nestled in the quiet. Like all cherished havens, Christ-centred Friends may come to believe that this tranquillity belongs to them alone. Here the canopy of divine grace becomes a delicate private possession, to be guarded against the unjust intrusions of the non-Christian world. Indeed, like the ancient faithful obscured in the catacombs, such Friends may begin to see the world outside not merely as a diversion, but a covert enemy of Christ's many gifts. In this defensive posture, Jesus is held close to the chest like a delicate porcelain doll. The greatest fear here is that a gust from the outside world could cause this holy figurine to topple and smash. Given the harsh conditions of indifferent secularity under which many Christ-centred Quakers live, the posture is doubtless understandable, but it is profoundly distorting of the Quaker understanding of Jesus. Jesus Christ needs neither protection, nor a line drawn around him to sustain his integrity. When Christians say 'Jesus is Lord' they mean to say that the whole world, past, present, and future, belongs to Christ alone. He is not an alien factor in history, nor does he need to be fenced in. He is the one of whom it was said

> every knee should bow,
> in heaven and on earth and under the earth,
> and every tongue acknowledge that Jesus Christ is Lord,
> to the glory of God the Father. (Philippians 2:10–1)

The divine life that beats in Jesus is not fragile, nor is it easily muddied by the compromises and confusions of the world, since all things find their ultimate home in Christ's heart; believers and deniers, saints and sinners, insiders, and outsiders. If we wish to restore and sustain this truly universal vision of Christ, we need to tease out the contemporary implications of foundational Quaker conceptions of Church and worship. In an attempt to explain to themselves how they came to gather in silent waiting, the first Friends returned again and again to the pouring out of the Spirit at Pentecost. As Acts 2 depicts the scene:

> When the day of Pentecost came, they [the disciples] were all together in one place. Suddenly a sound like the blowing of a violent wind came from heaven and filled the whole house where they were sitting. They saw what seemed to be tongues of fire that separated and came to rest on each of them. All of them were filled with the Holy Spirit and began to speak in other tongues as the Spirit enabled them. (Acts 2: 1–4)

But the Spirit did not stop there. Descending upon a vast crowd of 'Parthians, Medes, and Elamites; residents of Mesopotamia, Judea and Cappadocia, Pontus and Asia, Phrygia, and Pamphylia, [and] Egypt', the assembled people began to understand one another's language. While the original Jewish feast of Pentecost commemorated the giving of the Law at Sinai, Luke–Acts re-interprets this event through the lens of the Risen Christ. In place of the ethnically specific authority of the Torah, the post-Pentecost Church was to be governed by the Law of the Spirit (in which authority is invested in an ethnically mixed community of believers, drawn from the ends of the world). While the human family before Christ had been hopelessly divided by country, language and cult, the world after the Messiah would possess in his Church, the embryonic template for a new global community of peace and justice. Taking this image to heart, the first Quakers emphasised the inclusive actions of the Spirit as seen in the early Church. Core to this commitment was the acknowledgement that the work of the Spirit went far beyond the bounds of the Church and Israel. Christ could, in principle, dwell in and work in all. When William Penn spoke of the 'humble, meek, merciful, just and devout souls' being 'everywhere of one religion'[110] he was stating, what was to him, an obvious spiritual fact about the work of Christ and his Church. The same can be said of the fondly quoted statement by Fox that 'Christ hath enlightened ... the Turks, Jews, and Moors'.[111] In this respect, Friends stayed faithful, not merely to the message of Pentecost but to a vivid streak of cosmopolitanism in the Hebrew Scriptures, which saw the Spirit of God as working through unlooked for and startling avenues. We have the story of the Gentile prophet Balaam, who despite his desire to curse Israel, finds himself becoming God's spokesman.[112] Similarly, we have the Persian King Cyrus, who, despite the wrongs done to the Jews by his imperial might, becomes God's preferred instrument for restoring Jewish nationhood.[113] The importance of these strange moments lies in their paradigmatic nature. In their apparent incongruity, they reveal something fundamental about the nature and action of Christ. Despite the division of the human race along tribal, ideological, and political lines, God sees these distinctions for the phantoms they really are. It is the power of the unexpected, boundary-crossing God that animated early Friends in their Witness and Worship.

How should this radical ecclesiology guide how contemporary Christ-centred Friends live their lives? Like much early Quaker theology, contemporary Christian Friends will find much consolation and challenge in equal measure. To say that the world is Christ's, and that his Spirit crosses boundaries, is to invite hope midst despair. In a world divided by nationality, politics, and faith, we are summoned to the task of creating a just peace. But the lesson of Pentecost is double-edged in that it challenges some of our most precious beliefs about community and belonging. Christ-centred Friends are by no means excluded from such radical questioning. Perhaps the most persistent emotion among Christians in the Religious Society of Friends is a profound lack of belonging. In contrast to the early Quaker vision of a universal Spirit-led Church, such Friends may lament the existence of the many distinct Quakerisms now jostling for recognition. Perhaps the greatest exponent of the Quaker-Christian theory of loss was the American Friend Lewis Benson (1906–1986). A stern critic of the generic mysticism of Rufus Jones, Benson observed what he regarded as the gradual decline of a shared Christian understanding within un-programmed Meetings. With this loss of a Christ-rooted centre, Benson saw Friends becoming a pale shadow of their former selves, disparate and lacking spiritual vitality. Where once Friends had possessed a clear sense of both Christ and God, modern Liberal Quakers were wholly bereft of the Society's former inspiration, filling the theological gaps with theosophical and perennial appeals to non-confessional inward religion. This liberalisation and diversification culminated, according to Benson, in the desire to detach Quakerism from Christianity altogether. Surveying the character of this Post-Christian Quakerism in 1984, Benson lamented:

[In] England there is a Quaker Universalist Group, at least some of whom are dedicated to eliminating the Christian content from Quaker thought and experience, on the grounds that this content is secondary and therefore expendable, and I have no doubt that there will be Quakers in the United States who will make a favorable response to this concern. In my own yearly meeting in New York it became a matter of policy a few years ago to accept into membership applicants who make no profession of faith in Jesus Christ, so that there is now a sizable number of members who are not professing Christians. The yearly meeting has been busily engaged in recent years in revising its book of Faith and Practice so that it will serve the needs of both its Christ-centered members and its non-Christ-centered members.[114]

On the face of it, Benson is right. There is a growing number of Friends who wish to eliminate Christian language and theology altogether from the structure of Quakerism. Indeed, I have met many such Friends in my travels within the Society. But I continue to wonder whether Benson was right in his overall pessimism, that it is the breaking of Quakerism's Christian fence which is at the root of our problems. After all, people of other confessions, Methodists, Catholics, Anglicans, and Baptists, make similar complaints about the loss of spiritual vitality, and yet they have few in their communities who would explicitly define themselves against Christian identity. Could it be that the deep-seated problem at the heart of Liberal Quakerism is not our lack of boundaries, but our lack of trust in the gathering Spirit contained in our story? This trust contains within it the rather unfashionable notion of providence, that all times and places express the deep structure of a divine will, under which all events can in principle be fitted together. This puts a sharp challenge to self-described Christ-centred Quakers. Are such Friends so enmeshed in a theory of Christian loss that they no longer believe that God can bring order to diversity? Can such Friends affirm the Christ revealed at Pentecost and at the same time conclude that the non-Christian, the humanist, or the bystander cannot be called by Christ in a gathered Meeting? After all, as we see in the Pentecost episode, the power of the Spirit extended well beyond the Apostolic circle.

This fact goes to the very heart of what it means to follow Christ in an increasingly diverse Religious Society of Friends. In times of persecution and disorder, Friends built walls around the Society to survive, and to pass on the Quaker story to future generations. But these walls, a practical expediency, did not say anything theologically definitive about the God that early Friends worshipped. The One who called George Fox from despair, affirmed that His Spirit would be poured out 'on all flesh' (Joel 2:28). For early Friends, this commitment manifested most radically in their belief that infants and young children could fully participate in the experience of Worship. This inclusion of the very young was merely an extension of the ancient testimony of Israel, that unlikely persons, persons with wrong beliefs, or no beliefs in the case of very young children, may become agents of God's Kingdom. It is this commitment to the revolutionary generality of God's gifts that lie behind that otherwise baffling claim in Luke's Gospel that the future John the Baptist 'leaped' in his mother's, Elizabeth's, womb, being 'filled with the Holy Spirit' (Luke 1:41). If indeed the Spirit can use diverse and surprising containers to accomplish its earthly tasks, then it would be spiteful at best, and blasphemous at worst, to deny the possibility that Universalists, Theists, and Non-Theists can and do offer significant channels for the

Light. Indeed, as the examples of Balaam and Cyrus suggest, one's intentions or opinions are unimportant to the ultimate effectiveness of Jesus' call. To hone this point a little further, we might say (in the language of Pentecost) that while Non-Theists, Universalists or generic Quaker Theists speak their own particular religious language, the Spirit of God in its capacity as great translator, can render such speech intelligible within a gathered meeting. In framing their role in this way, I am not suggesting that such Friends are involuntarily helpful cuckoos in the Quaker nest. Rather, I propose that we each are a window into God's Kingdom, a fact which is not dependent upon the prior acceptance of particular theological or scriptural propositions. Indeed, as Doug Gwyn has vividly summarised this point:

> It is Fox's belief that the Word of God, unmediated by scripture, enlightens everyone, and that the Holy Spirit, according to the prophecy of Joel, is poured out on all flesh, even where the scriptures are not known or the gospel not preached. On his trip to America, Fox was able to explore this belief through conversations with the Indians. His question to them was simple – did they know something within them which reproved them when they did wrong? He concluded that all know this experience and that it was Christ's light.[115]

Here one can observe the deep radicalism at the heart of the Quaker-Christian vision. *The Spirit is no discriminator of persons.* The only proper religious measure of the Spirit's activity is the individual's willingness to delve within and seek that voice which bids them to do 'what is just and right. Rescue from the hand of the oppressor the one who has been robbed. Do no wrong or violence to the foreigner, the fatherless or the widow' (Jeremiah 22:3). This is not to say that the story of Scripture is unimportant, only that God's teaching could not be obstructed by its absence. If we place this Christian universalism in conversation with contemporary Quaker pluralism, we are inclined to reject a view which says that belief guarantees the validity of one's religious life. The extent of God's action is not dependent upon our perceptions and initiative. Godself works in us regardless of what we choose to think about such work.

If non-Christian Quakers can be agents and portals of the Light, how do such Friends keep Christ-centred Quakerism faithful to itself? We might define the constructive role of these Friends in terms of inoculation against idolatry. To worship an idol is more than the act of venerating images of stone, metal, or wood. In the broader exegetical tradition of both Christianity and Judaism, idolatry signifies a sustained misdirection of energy, heart and feeling into the divinisation of that which is not itself divine: the veneration of economic systems, political parties, or ethnic affiliations. But perhaps the most insidious form of idolatry is the erroneous devotion of particular religious beliefs or ecclesial forms, under the mistaken belief that this is tantamount to worshipping God. In the case of Jesus, idolatry can manifest as a fixed notion of who Jesus is and what he thinks of us. Instead of listening to the Living Jesus in our hearts, we shut our heart to an ongoing relationship, preferring instead a digestible doctrine or precise account of Jesus rather than Christ Himself. It is here that both Universalists and Non-Theists offer valuable philosophical medicines to cure Christian Friends of this weakness. Perhaps the greatest virtue of Quaker Universalism in its many modern forms, is its resolute refusal to mistake a religious map for the spiritual territory. With their commitment to mystical immediacy and their suspicion of the primacy of a single spiritual story, Universalists warn Christ-centred Friends away from becoming too attached to a single way of describing Jesus or his work. In this decided distrust of finalities, fixities, and absolutes, Universalism encourages Christian Quakers to reserve some mystery to Jesus' person, preventing us from treating him as an object we can control, predict, or curry favour with. The sense that more can be known than can ever be said gives Jesus the space to be Jesus. To acknowledge that the force of words gives out at the feet of mystery is not a threat to the slow Quaker Jesus, but a way of affirming his immediate and unfurling essence. Since the Christocentric Friend worships a living Spirit, not an august statue, to be reminded of the inadequacy of one's ideas and images is always an important service. As Janet Scott observed in her Swarthmore Lecture of 1980: 'We must hold our symbols lightly, for as long as they are helpful but let them go as we seek new interpretations. For the power lies not in the symbols themselves but in the Spirit which they try to represent.'[116] If we are committed to this mode of seeking, attentive always to the reality behind our words (put less metaphysically, the real work they call us to do), the slow Jesus will live in us, not as a theory, much less a precious allegiance to be protected, but as a living personality. To recognise this quality of ongoing relationship is to affirm the possibility, not merely that the long-hallowed words we use about Jesus are meant to be applied in our contemporary conditions, but also that new words may arise in our conversation with Jesus. If we are to be more than a historical re-enactment society, we must be open to these new images not as invaders in an enclosed religious landscape, but as possible companions who can help us answer Jesus' question: 'Who do you say I am?' (Matthew 16:13–20).

A generous Christian Friend could perhaps grant that the slow Jesus is indeed served by the mysticism of Quaker Universalism. But in this faith of concrete relation, what possible purpose could non-Theism serve? If Universalism inoculates us from idealising any one image of Jesus, Quaker Humanism offers harsher medicine still. In the course of human history, conscientious objection to religious systems has played a crucial role in the refinement of our ideas about the world and our place in it. It has not only given space for the flourishing of human reason in the formation of social life, but rightly esteemed the humane values of inquiry and progress in the face of inflexible dogmas of all kinds. In the West, we have the ancient Greek Cynics and Epicureans who jointly objected to the incoherence and superstition at the heart of traditional religious belief and practice. Finding the anthropomorphic nature of the Greek pantheon a matter of amusement, Cynics mocked the cults, shrines, and petty rituals, intended to placate invented deities. Alongside the Cynic suspicion of fakery, the Epicureans were concerned that an uncritical worship of these creations would inevitably lead to self-serving fundamentalism – by which human dignity and autonomy are exchanged for fear, brutality, and delusion. When faced with the prospect of compromising the needs of human beings for some imagined sacred good, the voice of both Cynic and Epicurean Humanism remains decisive. We must stay rooted in the concrete, the personal and relational in the face of idols that demand sacrifice. Just as the Hebrew Prophets berated the community of Israel for their tendency to worship gods of their own fashioning, Quaker Non-Theism has the capacity to challenge Christian Friends to look more critically at their understanding of Jesus. Do Christocentric Quakers have any golden calves they refuse to challenge? When Christian Quakers speak of that Spirit which moves and guides them, do they seek the earth-shattering experience of early Friends, or are they content with pleasant fantasies, which, like a child's invisible playmates, are immune from criticism or accountability? Do such Friends ever place theological conviction beyond the flourishing of individuals or communities? These are old preoccupations for Quakers. In the mid-seventeenth century the London Quaker William Shewen warned those gathered in godly silence of that pretend worship which was nothing but 'will-worship, self-work and voluntary humility' that had 'no acceptance with God'.[117] In tackling the scourge of will-worship, Non-Theist Friends have much sober advice to offer Christians on how not to become captured by inadequate, dubious, or even juvenile constructions of the Divine that sow seeds of inhumanity, hardness, or moralism in an otherwise tender heart. Moreover, the generous humanism of such Friends, in its frequent appeal to ordinary reason, in its grounded-ness in the present moment, in its focus on the fruits of concrete actions, all prevent our talk of Christ becoming ethereal, otherworldly, or abstracted from pressing human needs. When such internal criticism is applied to our devotion with care and tenderness, nothing can rob the Jesus of our Quaker story of his power and dignity. While such sceptical deconstruction may very well rob us of our hubris, our lazy assumptions, or our cherished formulation, this is not the same as Jesus. All that is self-involved in our Jesus will doubtless die before the critical inquisitions of Quaker Non-Theism, but the slow Jesus will live ever more vitally, unshackled from the heavy burdens of artificial lines that pretend to tell us where Jesus is and where Jesus isn't.

Uncovering Christ-Shaped Universalism

Given the unruly and inclusive quality of the Christ of Quaker tradition, what have Quaker Universalists made of Jesus? In the illuminating 2007 collection *Universalism and Spirituality* published by the Quaker Universalist Fellowship, Richard Barnes suggests that post-Christian Universalism now constitutes the fundamental character of Liberal Quakerism. This new phase of Quaker life is characterised by Barnes as including a decisive shift away from an exclusive attachment to Christian tradition and an eager acknowledgement of a plurality of spiritual sources. Rejecting accounts of Quaker distinctiveness rooted in older assumptions of Christian religious chauvinism, Barnes observes:

Our Society is no longer simply another Christian denomination with Christ at its centre. No longer do we believe that the other religions revolve around us and our religion, but that our religion revolves around a Universal Centre. The Judeo-Christian tradition remains a major, but not the only, source of spiritual guidance. Our uniqueness and our source of identity as a religious body lie *not* in a commonly held set of religious beliefs or a theology.[118]

This project of decoupling Christianity from Quaker life has frequently put Universalist Friends in the position of gadflies, provoking a seemingly self-satisfied Christian Quakerism to defend both the uniqueness of Jesus' person and revelation. For most Universalists, however, the response of Quaker-Christian tradition to the dilemma of global religious diversity has been anything but convincing. Indeed, the person of Jesus has often served as shorthand for what Universalists regard as an outdated religious exclusivism. 'Why', asks Gene Kudsen Hoffman, 'is Jesus' injunction to love our enemies any more decisive than that of Lao-Tse, Socrates, or Gandhi? Why is a book from Palestine any more holy than a book from China, India, or America?'[119] In the light of such questions, the only course remaining to Liberal Universalism, other than outright rejection, has been to refashion Jesus into a marvellous mystagogue whose teachings transcend the time and place in which they were taught. Instead of being a byword for intolerance, Jesus is here placed in friendly conversation with Shakyamuni, Guru Nanak, and the sublime writer of the *Bhagavad Gita*. In this dialogical vein, Jesus the human sage can still be justly called 'the Son of God', if by this we mean a personality filled with Eternal Wisdom. This makes Jesus far from unique, but nonetheless important. If divinity is conferred by knowledge and not birth, then in principle, all can become Sons and Daughters of God. In this reading, the Gospel of Christ becomes one more paradigmatic example of spiritual truth, confirming, albeit in specific circumstances, what the

Liberal mystic already knows: that God is universal, inward, and absolutely One. But despite this perennial understanding, Jesus remains a deeply unnerving presence among Liberal Universalists in ways that Buddha, Nanak, and Krishna simply aren't. The source of this discomfort is doubtless rooted in the fact that the story of Jesus cannot be disconnected from the unique claims that are made about Him. To encounter Jesus is to confront certain facts that force one to make a marked choice between Jesus and others. In Christ's orbit it is not possible to hold that all mystical claims are in some sense true, since the New Testament repeatedly claims that Christ represents the decisive revelation of God in the human world: 'I am the way and the truth and the life. No one comes to the Father except through me' (John 14:6). These assertions, if taken seriously, not merely upset the comfortable Universalist contention that all revelations are made equal, but the intersecting claim that no one personality or body of teaching can adequately symbolize the entirety of spiritual truth. What then is the Liberal Universalist to do? Is Jesus to be accepted? Muted? Thrown out? An answer to this dilemma is provided by the *slow Jesus* of our Quaker Way. As with our last discussion, the Christ at the very centre of our worship brings both gifts and challenges for the Universalist inquirer. Those who desire a hospitable approach to interreligious understanding will find much in the way of riches. But for those who wish to individualise and de-historicise the spiritual quest, the Jesus of Quaker tradition offers nothing but a stern repudiation. How should we make sense of this apparent contradiction? Let's start untying this Gordian knot by mapping out the distinctive character of the early Quaker account of Christ among the religions.

Reflecting on the inclusive character of Quaker theology in the late-seventeenth century, William Penn argued that the Light that Friends worshipped was nothing less than the Eternal Word who had latterly become flesh in the life of the iterant Jewish preacher Jesus of Nazareth. But as Penn was keen to stress, this Heavenly Word had lived in others. Classical pagans like Heraclitus, Socrates, Plato, Sophocles, Plutarch, and Plotinus, while never hearing the Gospel preached, had nonetheless tasted the Eternal love of Christ. In a beautiful letter addressed to his children, Penn summarised this perspective by offering multiple names for the Godhead:

> I have chosen to speak in the language of the scripture; which is that of the Holy Ghost, the spirit of truth and wisdom, that wanted no art or direction of man to speak by; and express itself fitly to man's understanding. But yet that blessed principle, the eternal word I begun with to you, and which is that light, spirit, grace and truth, I have exhorted you to in all its holy appearances of manifestations in your selves, by which all things were at first made, and man enlightened to salvation, is Pythagoras's great light and salt of ages, Anaxagoras's divine mind, Socrates's good spirit, Timaeus's unbegotten principle, and author of all light, Hieron's God in man; Plato's eternal, ineffable, and perfect principle of truth; Zeno's maker and father of all; and Plotin's root of the soul.[120]

These trajectories naturally led Penn towards a radical mode of interreligious hospitality which explicitly rejected the notion of automatic Christian superiority, and instead sought to rehabilitate the wisdom of the pre-Christian past. In the company of the virtuous ancients, Penn found himself lamenting 'how little the Christians of the times are true philosophers, and how much more these philosophers were Christian than they, let the Righteous Principle in every conscience judge. But then is it not intolerable that they should be esteemed Christians who are yet to learn to be good Heathen'.[121] Penn's attitude was clear. One's assent to the outward religion of Christianity was not enough to establish one's spiritual validity in the eyes of

God. Each had a responsibility to look inside themselves for the Living Water that had once quenched Jesus and the Prophets. All who came to this inner fountain belonged to the Church, whatever their external condition or confessional label. There is doubtless something deeply comforting for most Quaker Universalists in such a charitable exposition. After all, it suggests the kind of boundless mystical unity, which is so attractive to non-confessional moderns. Indeed, a cursory reading of Penn might imply a kind of Christ-tinged polytheism, in which Jesus appears contentedly as one star among many, shining in a constellation of spiritual teachers. But such a concept is altogether too cosy, too blurred by our modern preoccupations with multiculturalism, hybridity, and liberal tolerance, to be authentically Quaker. In many respects the early Quaker vision of Christ was altogether more radical than the rather tame Liberal Jesus of so much latter-day perennialism. What is so often missing in post-Christian Universalism is a willingness to inhabit two early Quaker paradoxes that offer keys to the way Friends spoke and believed. The first tension Friends lived daily was the notion that the universal is revealed in the particular. The God who dwelt with Friends had a common revelation for all people, but that universal message always appeared in specific places, for specific individuals. These historical contingencies were, however, never obscurers of the truth. Rather, the details of context (events and persons) were how divine revelation was revealed to contingent and time-bound hearers. Following the prophetic logic of Scripture, Friends regarded history as the chief vessel of the Eternal. The second tension concerned Friends' profound sense that Christ both judges all religions and upholds the religious impulses of all people. The Light which Friends worshipped dwelt in all, and upheld the dignity of all, and yet revealed the manifold ways in which selves dwelt in untruth and darkness. People possessed spiritual reality within them, and yet they found it nearly impossible to find. When both paradoxes were held as equally crucial, they allowed early Friends to argue for a Universal religion, while keeping firmly within the bounds of Christian faith.

How then should we understand the claim that the universal is to be found in the particular? For Penn, Christ's universality did not mean that the Inward Light was without anchor or context. The God revealed from Heraclitus to Jesus was not some vague principle of inward truth divorced from the past, but a divine life with a unique temperament and a distinct story. This sense of God as 'person' stemmed from the sense, (preserved in both Jewish and Greek Scripture) of religious experience as an encounter, a Reality which loved, remembered, wept, and even raged. Thus, God enters the human world not as pure transcendence, but as turbulent bouts of feeling, wrestling, and desiring. This decidedly relational character is revealed first and foremost in the people of Israel, a community set aside as peculiar beacons of a universal divine light in a world that remains largely indifferent to God. In this way, Jesus is more than a homely Liberal sage. He is a bearer of this record and an expositor of this vocation. Liberal Universalists are wrong if they think the affirmation of radical diversity depends upon the downgrading of Jesus' uniqueness. Early Friends found precisely the opposite. The more they centred their lives in the particularities of Jesus' life, death, and Resurrection, the more they were able to understand a larger life and a more expansive history. Instead of generalising Christ's revelation to the point of meaninglessness, Penn's Universalism would have us be attentive to Jesus' fundamental specificity. Where should we begin? The first step in this process is to redeem from obscurity the spiritual illumination offered by Jesus' context. The man Jesus was not a religious statue, an immovable angel, or a disembodied Great Soul, but a son, a friend, a brother, who lived and died in a Jewish world. His home and country were circumscribed by the sacred dramas of the Exodus, the giving of the Torah, and the Hebrew entry into the Promised Land. His day was punctuated by the rhythms of prayer and cultic purification. He was born the son of a people and died with the words of that people on his lips. What is the significance of this Christ 'from somewhere'? Jesus' Jewishness, so often seen as an irrelevant contingency among Universalists, should be a sign to us that we are called, not to be isolated walkers on an ahistorical journey, but builders of a life together, rooted in the worship of that God who dwelt with Abraham, Jacob, and Moses.

Such a vocation does not negate the fact that we live, love, and discover in a world full of religions, only that our spiritual tasks 'begin somewhere' and that they possess a positive shape which transcends our individual preferences. Jesus' title of 'Messiah' tells us that the God at the centre of the religious endeavour is concerned, not with individual spiritual growth, but the transformation of the world after the pattern of Israel, a community rooted in the logic of thankfulness, worship, and Sabbath. In Jesus, we see the trust of Abraham and the blessing of Jacob becoming shared possessions, for the whole human family. Such a conception is a gentle challenge to the post-Christian Universalist who worries about the insulating effects of inhabiting a single story. Intolerance can be fostered by unthinking pluralism just as much as unyielding sameness. The key to religious generosity is whether the stories we tell have the capacity to include others, cross boundaries and build bridges. In the case of Jesus, his narrative is not closed, but tantalizingly porous. This structure is beautifully signified in Matthew's story of the journeying Magi, (Matthew 2:1–12). These priests of the Zoroastrian faith, thought in antiquity to be mighty astrologers and formidable sorcerers, did not belong to Israel's story, but they were nonetheless drawn into it by their faith's own promise of a cosmic Saviour (Saoshyant) who would bring about the restoration of the world. Thus, the story of Christ does not simply divide people into believers and unbelievers, but is continuingly calling outsiders to itself, in an effort to fulfil their deepest hopes. This call to generous community, rooted in a single story, draws us to the second paradox of early Quakerism, namely Christ's judgement on all religions. In the last century, the most robust examiner of this theme was the Reformed theologian Karl Barth (1886–1968). For Barth, all human religious forms sat under the judgement of Jesus Christ. Their worth depended not upon a list of correct beliefs or positions, but rather on whether they looked to themselves or the Living God for guidance and justification. Were the sacred systems of a given culture open to the possibility of divine judgement? Or did such frameworks attempt to presage such a fateful decision by judging and vindicating themselves in advance? Contrasting such spiritual egotism with the absolutely free act of divine self-disclosure, Barth argued that:

> [Religion contradicts revelation] because truth can come to man only through the truth. If man grasps at the truth on his own, then of necessity it eludes his grasp. So he does not do what he would have to do when the truth comes to him. So, then he does not have faith. If he had faith he would listen; but in religion he talks. If he had faith he would allow something to be given to him, but in religion he takes something for himself. If he had faith he would let God himself stand up for God; but in religion he dares that grasping after God. Because it is this grasping, religion is the contradiction of revelation, the concerted expression of the human lack of faith, that is the attitude and activity, directly opposed to faith.[122]

In this respect, Barth offers a strikingly psychological account of human religiosity by explaining the diversity of sacred allegiances, doctrines, and positions, appealing to the polymorphic nature of human longing. If God's self-disclosure constitutes the radical breaking-in of a single incontestable reality, then religion stemmed from a human desire to muddy its starkness, tame its absoluteness, and pre-empt its verdict. Under the auspices of religion, the world was made safe for the most elaborate of cultural fantasies. Christ stood in judgement on all these facsimiles, revealing them to be shadows of living religion, given and authored by God alone. In positing this argument, Barth noted that 'it was not possible to attribute to Christianity a special position, a place protected from every judgement'.[123] The lesson of the Reformation, exemplified by Luther and Calvin, was that Christians could become just as ensnared in self-serving religiosity as non-Christians. Perennial temptations for the follower of Christ included an obsession with works, an exaggerated attachment to ecclesial outward forms, and the use of piety to obscure egotism. These recurrent failures implied for Barth a profound posture of humility when confronting the religions of others. Instead of turning our attention outwards to the false religiosity of outsiders, Barth suggests that:

[It] is incumbent upon us precisely as Christians to allow this judgement to apply first and most acutely to ourselves and to others, the non-Christians, only to the extent that we recognize ourselves in them, i.e. that we recognise that the truth of this judgement of revelation applies to us and encounters us – and thus in a solidarity, in which we, anticipating them in repentance and hope, submit ourselves to this judgement, in order thereby also to participate in the promise of revelation.[124]

Those seeking a vivid summary of early Quaker preaching will find Barth's analysis illuminating. The notion that Christ had called time on human religion was a theme expressed again and again by George Fox in his initial preaching. For early Friends, Quakerism was not merely *another way to Worship*, it was an attempt to free people from their manifold projections of God, from hollow steeple-houses, empty rituals, and false worships. Christ was bigger than any human attempt to grasp, tame, or pre-empt him. In this respect, first-generation Quakers reserved their harshest criticisms for a smug Christendom that fixated on useless images and airy constructions, rather than the vital movements of the Spirit. True enough, there were many people in the world who did not know the teaching of Christ, and in time they should be brought to the Light in themselves. But Friends thought it more urgent that Christians should walk faithfully with Jesus before they set about telling others about him. In this way, Quaker-Christian Universalism has always strolled some way in the path Barth latterly sketched. But early Friends added something to this picture of 'religion under judgement' that Barth had under-explored, namely the presence of God's *truth, even midst untruth*. For Barth, Jesus' self-revelation demonstrates that, generally speaking, religion is false, becoming true only insofar as God acts within the confines of religion to bring people to Himself. In this vein, Barth was careful to say that 'Jesus Christ does not somehow augment or improve human attempts to conceive and present God by human standards; rather as God's self-offering, he replaces them, thereby simply surpassing them'.[125] But early Friends could not follow Barth in drawing such a sizeable chasm between human culture and Christ. The Light taught early Friends that God directly entered human culture, and in doing so, not merely toppled it, but repaired it, even graced it. One thinks of William Penn's encounter with the Native Americans who sat with him in silence. These people knew the Way, they knew the right posture, they knew how to wait. Christ had already given them the blessing that others had arrogantly proclaimed to them. Certainly Barth conceded the possibility that non-Christian religions 'might have served as preparation for the proposition that the Christian religion is *true*'.[126] But as Penn's experience showed, the first Quaker communities went much further. However people lived, regardless of creed or language, Christ could be immediately available. Even those who stood against the Light could benefit from its illumination, whether Pagan or Christian, Jew or Muslim, believer or nonbeliever. The ubiquitous activity of the Light speaks to the early Quaker conviction that no human barrier could stand in the way of God's grace. This vision of God's generous breaking-in, had a significant impact on Quaker accounts of salvation. While other denominations pretended clarity regarding the division of 'saved' and 'unsaved', Quakers such as Robert Barclay held that, in principle, all could find their way to God. As he put it in his *Apology*:

> This doctrine of universal redemption, or Christ's dying for all men, is of itself so evident from the Scripture testimony that there is scarce found any other article of the Christian faith so frequently, so plainly, and so positively asserted. It is that which maketh the preaching of Christ to be truly termed the Gospel, or an annunciation of glad tidings to all. Thus the angel declared the birth and coming of Christ to the shepherds to be (Luke 2:10), "Behold, I bring you good tidings of great joy, which shall be to all people": he saith not to a few people. Now if this coming of Christ had not brought a possibility of salvation to all it should rather have been accounted bad tidings of great sorrow to most people; neither should the angel have had reason to have sung "Peace on earth and good will towards men" if the greatest part of mankind had been necessarily shut out from receiving any benefit by it.[127]

In this generous mode, Christ is not merely the one who holds the human-centred religions to account, He is the one who nestles himself in all religion, drawing strength even from those who oppose him. In this model of story-specific Universalism,

Christ has no need to subordinate religions to himself, to lessen the Other so that he becomes greater. All the religious contents of the human world are a tool for his glory. Even in idolatry, in the depths of pretence, Jesus will use doubtful materials to make headway in the heart. This expansive attitude is readily acknowledged in the biblical narrative itself, exemplified in the ministry of the Apostles Paul and Barnabas. After healing a man of lameness, the apostles are confronted with an adulated crowd:

> When the crowds saw what Paul had done, they lifted up their voices in the Lycaonian language: "The gods have come down to us in human form!" Barnabas they called Zeus, and Paul they called Hermes, because he was the chief speaker. The priest of Zeus, whose temple was just outside the city, brought bulls and wreaths to the city gates, hoping to offer a sacrifice along with the crowds. But when the apostles Barnabas and Paul found out about this, they tore their clothes and rushed into the crowd, shouting, "Men, why are you doing this? We too are only men, human like you. We are bringing you good news that you should turn from these worthless things to the living God, who made heaven and earth and sea and everything in them." (NIV Acts 14:11–14)

Something important should be drawn from this passage. Paul and Barnabas do not face a crowd of materialists, but encounter a culture that already expects the divine to work in their lives. Centuries of prayer and sacrifice to other gods have made them open to the Spirit of Christ. By dubbing Paul and Barnabas Zeus and Hermes, these spectators had in mind the ancient stories of divine epiphany, of gods garbed in the form of strangers to test the hospitality of a city. Here the Greek cosmos dovetails with the Jewish world of Paul and Barnabas, of the angelic vitiation to Abraham, and by degrees, the risen Son of God who takes on the likeness of the dilapidated stranger on the road to Emmaus,

(Luke 24:13–32). Here, one clearly sees the double aspect of revelation. The lightning bolt of Christ illuminates the darkness of error, but it will never burn away those cultural structures of imagination and perception that bring people closer to the truth. The crowd's misidentification of Paul and Barnabas both confirms a world they already comprehend, and unwittingly draws them into an experience which is altogether unknown. Even their error, that which Christ holds under judgement, brings them closer to God. The risen Jesus is both a departure and an echo of what has already been mythically glimpsed in their own stories.[128] In this way, the Gospel does not compete for space with other religions. Christ is not a religious proposition or structure among others, but the Light and Truth sitting at the heart of all things. Consequently, all love, all hope, all reverence, can be made active ingredients in the articulation of the Gospel. Putting this observation in more obviously Quaker terms, we might say the Light does not destroy, but uses whatever is to hand to teach, heal, and build up. The God who loves us does not desire the abolition of our stories but uses them to draw diverse lives to Godself. A beautiful articulation of the latter position was crafted in the last century by the Catholic writer J.R.R. Tolkien, who passed it on to his friend C.S. Lewis. In a letter to Arthur Greeves in 1931, Lewis wrote:

> Now the story of Christ is simply a true myth: a myth working on us in the same way as the others, but with this tremendous difference that it really happened: and one must be content to accept it in the same way, remembering that it is God's myth where the others are men's myths: i.e. the Pagan stories are God expressing Himself through the minds of poets, using such images as He found there, while Christianity is God expressing Himself through what we call 'real things'.[129]

Here the pre-Christian and non-Christian worlds are not a field of uncomplicated falsehood, but rich veins of wisdom, offering God many portals through which to communicate Godself to varied human hearts. Tolkien and Lewis found traces of Christ everywhere in archaic literature, in myths of the midwinter sun, in ancient cults of light and fertility, in the tales of heroes and gods. It was in the latter category that both found potent evidences of God's revelation at work. In the dying and rising gods of past ages in the stories of Adonis, Balder, and Bacchus, they sensed an echo of what the God of Jesus Christ desired for the world from the very beginning, a springtime unstained by the bitter memory of winter. In the minds of Tolkien and Lewis, the Word becoming flesh did not destroy the older myths, but rather satisfied them, by rendering once nebulous constellations of hope into a living faith grounded in history. In a culture suspicious of those with trust in a single story, Lewis, and Tolkien's interpretation of Jesus as *manifest myth* is a much-needed reminder of what Universalism can be. One need not succumb to religious relativism to find God in all. One does not need to give up exclusive convictions to include the lives of others. One does not have to render Jesus a teacher among others to make the love of the Gospel a reality.

Christ at the Edges: Non-Theism and the Secret Messiah

So far we have journeyed with a radically liquid Jesus, who refuses to be tied down by creeds, structures, or beliefs. This is a Christ who is forever crisscrossing boundaries and flouting our lazy dualisms of insider and outsider. What do Non-Theist Friends make of such a strange character? Like Liberal Universalists, there are many Humanist Quakers who continue to find Jesus an uncomfortable enigma. Most frequently the figure of Christ is confined to two interpretative boxes, that of the unbelievable and the judgemental. Sat in the first container,

Jesus appears as an arcane myth utterly disconnected from the real world. The one who comes 'to judge the living and the dead' might as well be the Roman god Mithras, or more parochially, the tooth fairy. It is impossible to have strong feelings about such a fantastical figure one way or the other. In the second box, often filled with the primal emotions of childhood, Jesus manifests as a forbidding Superego who deploys shame and blame to accomplish his objective of 'saving souls'. This is the Jesus of the pointed finger and the fiery pit who is not beneath the threat of perpetual torture to elicit love (or at least the religious equivalent of Stockholm Syndrome). But as with most extreme depictions, these readings of Jesus are too simplistic to stand up to scrutiny. Jesus is neither fanciful mystery nor manipulative monster, but something far richer. My central argument in the final part of this chapter is that our Quaker Jesus, (the slow Messiah who resists naive totalities) should be regarded as both a beloved champion and challenger to Non-Theist Friends. As I will go on to show, an appreciation of the decidedly humanistic concerns at the heart of Christ's ministry reveals an earthy, practical personality, who refutes the suggestion that religion is identical with 'isms', abstracts, or repeated appeals to sublime transcendence. Instead, Jesus challenges Quaker Humanists to make their convictions truly effective by being *more* attached to the task of repairing and cherishing that which is fragile and human. Here, God's Paradise is found emmeshed between hands that welcome and arms that embrace. The Kingdom, as the Gospels tell us, is already in our midst. This is not a utopian project premised upon a new kind of human being. It takes us as we are by conceiving of the paradisical as simple acts of kindness, repeated care, and faithful welcome. How might this sacralisation of the present be achieved? Before speaking too grandly on this theme, let's first ground the task in an experience common to most Friends, the spectre of spiritual malaise. In her 2007 Swarthmore Lecture,

Beth Allen explored a recurrent temptation among Friends, the divinization of Quaker institutional life to the neglect of spiritual depth. Writing of her own experience of undertaking central Quaker work, Allen reflected:

> We have spent years, decades, trying to perfect our organization and our methods, and naturally cherish the community and the institution we have built. This is the failing of every single religious institution, however loving and holy the people who try and keep it going. The corporate body becomes a purpose in itself. Francis Howgill warned us: "If you build upon anything or have confidence in anything which stands in time and is on this side of eternity and the Being of Beings, your foundation will be swept away."[130]

Such institutionalisation is certainly a shared Quaker peril, but perhaps presses with particular intensity upon Non-Theist Quakers. After all, such Friends do not have the metaphysical luxury of falling back upon a God who offers an external vantage or standard from which to judge or qualify their formal Quaker allegiances. Allen tells Friends facing difficulty in their Meeting communities to affirm 'a fundamental, tested belief in God'.[131] But for most Non-Theists, there is no world under the skin of Quaker institutions that justifies them when they falter or gives them added momentum when they fail. There is certainly nothing like Allen's sense of God, 'the energy flowing through all the created universe ... transcendent yet, loving yet full of truth, eternal, outside time, yet working in time'.[132] Within the bounds of Quaker Humanism, there is no ultimate observer who keeps a beleaguered Friend attached to some essential but imperceptible Quaker core, when all about them appears in disrepair. There is no 'invisible Church', only what we visibly do, with and for one another. In this empirical account of Quaker life, Meeting communities stand or fall sociologically, that is, on the basis of connection, empathy, and skilfulness. By necessity, Non-Theists are creatures of exaggerated orthopraxy, cherishing the available Quaker furniture to apply and articulate their deepest values. But such a technique of self-creation is always double-edged. Living by practice alone is fruitful when one's experience of Meeting is vibrant and life-giving. But when our Quaker community becomes something burdensome or deeply dissatisfying, such Friends may feel a sense of failure. They may conclude that the only course is to lay down their responsibilities or even put physical distance between themselves and the source of their disillusionment. Merely clutching at Quaker practices or institutions ever more tightly seems to lead nowhere.

What is the proper remedy for disillusionment when emotional intelligence and self-creation give out? Part of the answer to such a quandary involves recognising that Quakerism is more than a behavioural creed. Being Quaker involves being embedded in a story that grounds and makes sense of our practices. Indeed, what we do and how we do it, makes little sense without this prior storyline. Whether we treat the Quaker story as symbolic or factual, as spiritual inspiration or empirical record, is secondary. The urgent question is: How are we going to live through the story? As I've argued in this book, the Quaker narrative is inseparable from the larger biblical plot, and more specifically, cannot be separated from the person of Jesus. In this sense, Christ is not just some strange supernatural addition to our traditions, but an active leavening agent that helps to turn our personal experience and practice into something which can nourish us. He is the One who is seen loving us from within. He is not a faraway divine king, but an immediate companion who offers us ways to walk. Such imminence provides Quaker Humanists with the first step in their quest for belonging midst the debris of stifling structures. The Jesus of Quaker memory bids those Friends who feel crushed by outer organisation to root down in the present. The Christ of our faith is not bound up with a faraway Deity, but depends upon cultivating transformative relationships in the now. Something of this pragmatic concreteness is preserved in the Gospel of Mark, where Jesus is confronted regarding the lax religious conduct of his disciples:

> One Sabbath, Jesus was going through the grainfields, and as his disciples walked along, they began to pick some heads of grain. The Pharisees said to him, "Look, why are they doing what is unlawful on the Sabbath?" He answered, "Have you never read what David did when he and his companions were hungry and in need? In the days of Abiathar the high priest, he entered the house of God and ate the consecrated bread, which is lawful only for priests to eat. And he also gave some to his companions." Then he said to them, "The Sabbath was made for man, not man for the Sabbath. So the Son of Man is Lord even of the Sabbath." (Mark 2:23–28)

Here, religiosity is not about sacrificing genuine needs to some unbending, otherworldly abstract. Rather, true faith is concerned with the enhancement of concrete human circumstances. Ritually honouring God's rest is not more important than weary people seeking rest. In this task, Jesus comes to us, not as a purveyor of sacred doctrine, but of practical relationships. Jesus' Messianic status is established far more by what he does, (the love he exhibits and the care he shows) than by what he claims. Thus, we are justified in thinking of Jesus as far more humanistic than we have been taught to suppose. Jesus' evident groundedness is powerfully expressed in his repeated posture of *prophetic marginality*. In the earliest of the Synoptic Gospels, Jesus the healing preacher and Messiah, never works out in the open. The barebones narrative of Mark possesses no glittering Nativity narrative, no celestial visitation to weary shepherds, no star proclaiming the fulfilment of age-old prophecy. There is only a man working in anonymity, often un-thanked and misunderstood. Few recognise who he is and those who do are often told by Jesus not to reveal his identity. Jesus even silences a demon who threatens to bring the full meaning of his work to the light of day (Mark 1:23–24). His disciples remain baffled throughout his ministry. Even when the signs of the old prophets are reproduced in flashing moments of Nativity-like clarity, his followers are left wondering, 'Who then is this, that even the wind and the sea obey him?' (Mark 4:41). In a beautifully enigmatic scene, we are told that:

> Jesus and his disciples went on to the villages around Caesarea Philippi. On the way he asked them, "Who do people say I am?" They replied, "Some say John the Baptist; others say Elijah; and still others, one of the prophets." "But what about you?" he asked. "Who do you say I am?" Peter answered, "You are the Messiah." Jesus warned them not to tell anyone about him. (Mark 8:27–29)

Jesus and his disciples were in a peculiarly ambiguous position. They noticeably healed, but they were unseen by much of the wider world. They were largely unknown to the priests in their Temple or the rulers in their villas. The disciples served but they were hidden in plain sight. They had no ritual apparatus, no power base, no majestic court in which to conduct their business. All they possessed were their bodies, hands, and feet, ready to heal and care. Their beloved teacher laboured for the Kingdom of God, but that Kingdom always broke out in patches, in lives healed, in persons restored. What Mark offers us is not some triumphant march of a spiritual revolution, but many fragmentary episodes of wonder which were frequently obscured by obstinate observers who refused to acknowledge what is happening in front of them. People shrugged, but at the same time 'the news about Him went out everywhere into all the surrounding district of Galilee' (Mark 1:28). The God in these encounters has no need for the trappings of outward glory, priests, temples, edifices of holy mediation, but works patiently at the margins, often unnoticed and unappreciated by the majority. This was often the posture adopted by early Friends too. Like their wandering Master, early Quakers would often go out into the world, their bodies and sense of mission, the only visible signs of their identity. How might this pose of simple and holy anonymity help contemporary Quaker Non-Theists in contesting their discouragement? These stances offer us vital spiritual guidance when the habits of institutional Quakerism feel altogether empty. Jesus' work in the shadows illustrates that living a grander life is not the same as smoothly fitting into a larger structure. Indeed, such structures can sometimes actively stand in the way of such a life insofar as it confuses love with institutional conformity or 'doing our duty'. We must look for another category of moral experience which transcends mere automatic practice, namely the small acts of spontaneous tenderness that keep us human. As the Jewish philosopher Emmanuel Levinas once put it:

> [T]he "small goodness" from one person to his fellowman is lost and deformed as soon as it seeks organization and universality and system, as soon as it opts for doctrine, a treatise of politics and theology, a party, a state, and even a church. Yet it remains the sole refuge of the good in being. Unbeaten, it undergoes the violence of evil, which, as small goodness, it can neither vanquish nor drive out.[133]

How do we loosen this *small goodness* from the hollow platitudes and burdens of routinised frameworks? How do we make kindness sacramental again? If Meeting is beginning to feel like a Temple that exists to uphold its own priestly reputation or processes, don't come to Meeting to 'do Quakerism', but come for the possibility of personal encounter, without the expectation of thanks or reward. Don't look to build or achieve anything, beyond being present and let what happens, happen. *Be human.* When we read the Gospels, we find in Jesus a stunning indifference to organisational structures or anything that we might latterly call 'a church'. Jesus' Messianic action began, not with big plans or efficient undertakings, but with personal attentiveness and openness to the guidance of the Spirit. The shape of Jesus' heart was coloured by the fields and villages of his home. He spoke in the accent of its joys and intimate tragedies, its little happenings, and its considerable scarcities. He was present for feasts and mourning. He saw weddings and dyings, bright faith, and dark despair. He was soaked in every deep shade of the human experience, not by transcending his time and place, but by sinking down into it. Begin at home, he seems to say. That is enough. When early Friends tried to express this imperative, they settled on the language of *tenderising* the heart. Gathering in the Spirit meant more than having a sublime experience. It meant becoming more compassionate, warm, and sympathetic towards the lives of others. This generous approach certainly helps Non-Theists be the best Humanists they can be, but it also challenges some bad habits. When more explicitly spiritual Quakers grumble that their Meetings are morphing into secular pressure groups or political organizations, the complaint attempts to articulate a fundamental obscuration of narrative logic to which Quaker Humanists are particularly prone. Being rooted 'in this world and its problems' is not the same as uncritically adopting the assumptions of secular politics and economics (no matter how laudable) as synonymous with our Quaker Way. Our primal vocabulary of love, grace and Spirit should encourage us to draw a line between what we are able to say and what the wider world says. Our life as Quakers is informed by a trust and a social imaginary which stands against instrumentalism, the supremacy of impact, and an obsession with usefulness that characterises the modern world. Meeting for Worship is not *for our values*. It is not a workplace, a committee, or a club for activists. Allen has astutely identified this subtle form of secularisation in terms of 'official' Quaker seriousness:

> When we Quakers become over-serious and over-busy, we risk a blighting barrenness of the spirit. We may not drink at all or rarely to excess, we don't overeat; one Quaker conference I organised was criticized because the food was too good and at another, a representative muttered, "my monthly meeting doesn't pay me to come to these events to enjoy myself."[134]

But if we cannot enjoy the simple fellowship of being gathered in love, what can we enjoy? The present writer readily admits that he is an incurable sensualist, but I suspect this posture is on spiritually safer ground, certainly more life-giving than a stilted office culture under the guise of a Meeting community.[135] In the face of the grey productivism of the wider world, we would do well to return to the Christ who is Lord of the Sabbath, of whom critics said: 'Here is a glutton and a drunkard, a friend of tax collectors and sinners' (Matthew 11:19). Our Meeting-life is not just another target driven company. *It is Sabbath*, it is rest and refreshment, it is graced time, a space in which we can 'just be', and a space in which to love. It is not about outcomes. It is about waiting and being surprised by the joy of waiting. In this regard, our Quaker Way is not merely on the side of religion's most esteemed contemplatives but is in accord with the loving instincts of that great English Humanist E.M. Forster. Writing at the end of the ideologically polarised 1930s, Forster despaired at the widespread uninterest in simple human intimacy and a corresponding preference for grand projects and anonymous political organizations. As Forster notes:

> Personal relations are despised today. They are regarded

as bourgeois luxuries, as products of a time of fair weather which is now past, and we are urged to get rid of them, and to dedicate ourselves to some movement or cause instead. I hate the idea of causes, and if I had to choose between betraying my country and betraying my friend, I hope I should have the guts to betray my country.[136]

Forster's praise of friendship midst the barrenness of machine politics and unyielding collectivities, should remind those who walk as 'Friends' that Meeting is made for human beings, not human beings for Meeting. If we follow Jesus' example of working at the edges of things, we discover that our hands and feet are all that is required to be authentically Quaker. We are not called to be institutionally 'useful', visible, or even sociable in the sense of 'clubbable'. To conflate Quakerism with these narrow social virtues is surely to leave us exhausted with Meeting when storm clouds come. If we wish to weather the storms of institutional deadness, we need a sturdier project rooted in the power of personal encounter. Let's seek genuine Friendship. Let's be immersed in the simple exchange, in welcoming the stranger, in trusting our most devoted stirrings. There is no better way of being dedicated to the generous Humanism of the slow Jesus.

Heaven: Walking the Road with Anne Conway

The Loss of Heaven

When placed in the context of eternity, what do our fleeting lives mean? Remarkably perhaps, this is not a subject contemporary British Friends commonly dwell on. A cursory exploration of our modern condition explains why. With its constant declarations of individual autonomy and the primacy of personal experience, Liberal Quakerism frequently leaves the individual alone with this existential quandary, precisely at those moments when a shared vision of existence is most sorely needed. When our lives are hounded by meaninglessness, brokenness, or tragedy, we rightfully seek out words and stories to make sense of our pain. But in its hyper-Liberal form, contemporary Quakerism has largely privatised this task, pushing ultimate things to the very margins of spiritual life. We have done this for myriad reasons, from pragmatism, from uncertainty, even from sheer awkwardness. This has led to a veil being thrown over our traditional talk of Judgement, Heaven, and the soul, to the detriment of our shared Quaker story. We frequently tell enquirers that Friends do not obsess over questions of eternity, but would rather focus upon living well in the present. Such an attitude has value up to a point. Too many minds have been captured by the allure of Eternity to the visible neglect of *this world*. In its most extreme form, such a mindset encourages a denial of life's value under the guise of religious seriousness. In the name of a spiritualised asceticism, such people selfishly turn their backs on a needful planet earth and look instead to the far shore of Heaven. In airy abstracts and lofty platitudes, they protect themselves from responsibility and the basic demands of compassion. Faced with this obvious extreme, Liberal Friends rightly return to the words of William Penn who gently chided:

> True godliness doesn't turn men out of the world, but enables them to live better in it, and excites their endeavours to mend it... Christians should keep the helm and guide the vessel to its port; not meanly steal out at the stern of the world and leave those that are in it without a pilot to be driven by the fury of evil times upon the rock or sand of ruin. (QF&P 23.02)

But *being in the world*, as Penn would have surely noted, is not the same as turning one's back on the reality of Heaven. There is so much nervous activism among contemporary Friends, nervous because such action is so often fuelled by the subconscious acceptance that this world is *all there is*. As a result, many Quakers feel a heavy responsibility to achieve concrete results, then feel disillusioned when their highest ideals fail to come to pass. Such disenchantment is a direct result of secularised lives that have been uncoupled from notions of Eternity. Friends enter struggles for justice and peace, forgetting that their lives are held within a larger reality that transcends their efforts. As the American Quaker Thomas R. Kelly once vividly expressed the problem:

> We are in an era of This-sidedness, with a passionate anxiety about economics and political organization. And the church itself has largely gone "this-sided" and large areas of the Society of Friends seem to be predominately concerned with this world, with time, and with the temporal order. And the test of the worthwhileness of any experience of Eternity has become: "Does it change things in time? If so let us keep it, if not, let us discard it." I submit that this is a lamentable reversal of the true order of dependence. Time is no judge of Eternity. It is the eternal who is the judge and taster of time.[137]

I have myself argued in this book that the fruit of practice is a good guide when attempting to live out our Quaker story, and so it is. But in saying this one must confront a beautiful contradiction. Certainly, our narrative and our practices are comprehended by their lived results, but our story also tells us that the Quaker Way would stand, even if we were somehow prevented from making the tree of faith bear a bountiful crop. This is because the path we walk is not about us, but instead concerns the Divine Centre we encounter in Worship. We honour our story most when we cease to grasp at it, when we stop expecting it to 'give us the goodies'. Our posture must always be: Not *my will, but your will be done*. Whether we fail or succeed on the shores of history, God's desire is never diverted. When we feel burnt out by the present, by the hard immediacy of things, we need to have this deeper world in our minds and hearts, not as an escape, but as a framework for our actions. Heaven is not, as early Friends knew, a distant place, it is the stream in which all things happen, the throbbing heart under the skin of the world. When we taste the sweetness and spice of Heaven, we finally understand the *why* of things. We sense that nothing we can do or say can diminish the grandeur of Being. We live here and now, but feel ourselves cloaked in time without end, and love without end. We recognise that, in the lap of God, we cannot fail to give goodness the room to grow. Centuries ago, Julian of Norwich expressed this deep sense of surety in the following way:

> And in this he showed me a little thing, the quantity of a hazel nut, lying in the palm of my hand, as it seemed. And it was as round as any ball. I looked upon it with the eye of my understanding, and thought, 'What may this be?' And it was answered generally thus, 'It is all that is made.' I marvelled how it might last, for I thought it might suddenly have fallen to nothing for littleness. And I was answered in

my understanding: It lasts and ever shall, for God loves it.
And so have all things their beginning by the love of God.[138]

These intuitions (and the images that go with them) are essential
to the structure of our Quaker Way, for from them comes our
hope in dark times. They take from our shoulders the misguided
belief that we and we alone must save things. It bids us trust a
Power beyond our striving and schemes, a love that transcends
all social visions or methods of political reform. Shortly before
his death in 1691, George Fox reflected: 'I am glad I was here.
Now I am clear, I am fully clear… All is well; the Seed of God
reigns over all and over death itself. And though I am weak
in body, yet the power of God is over all, and the Seed reigns
over all disorderly spirits' (QF&P 21.49). Like Julian before
him, Fox knew in his heart that, despite his infirmity, *all shall
be well, and all shall be well, and all manner of thing shall be well.*
Life could be lived in trust, despite brokenness and failure. How
do we contemporary Friends re-anchor ourselves in this hope?
In the proceeding pages, I turn to a neglected voice; the early
Quaker convert and philosopher Anne Conway (1631–1679).
I contend that among early Quaker writers, it is Conway's
approach to creation, redemption, and community, that can best
help contemporary Liberal Quakers integrate a sense of Eternity
into their daily lives. No simple purveyor of Heaven and Hell,
Conway imagined the Eternal world as a process of continuing
growth and renewal. God was not a Heavenly policeman, but
a fountain of perpetual love that sought to heal and refine all
times and all worlds. At the core of Conway's understanding of
existence was the recurring Quaker image of the Light shining in
the darkness (John 1:5). When Fox discovered the Light within
himself in the late 1640s, he understood the encounter as the mark
and herald of universal redemption. Christ had come to teach His
people Himself. Building on this theme of saving universality,
Conway treated Fox's Light as a paradigmatic image of a cosmic

situation, one in which even suffering was held in the gentle glow of divine love. For Conway, even life's toils represented a form of divine revelation, a disclosure which propelled each life and each creature closer to their completion in God. In this account, loss and failure are not charges against divine goodness, but rather the pangs of a new world coming to birth. In this vein, the image of Christ that most exercised Conway was the battered Lord adorned with a crown of thorns. Here, divinity was revealed not in strength and glory, but in weakness and subjection. It was this notion of theophany in wretchedness that structured Conway's most dazzling personal insights. Before considering these themes in detail, the opening part of this chapter offers an overview of Conway's life and thought, paying particular attention to her theological account of Eternity.

The Philosophy of Anne Conway

For the end is always like the beginning. (Origen, *First Principles* 6.2)

Like William Penn, Anne was born into privilege. She was the daughter of the noted Parliamentarian Sir Heneage Finch, and Elizabeth Cradock, the child of a prosperous London merchant family. As if to underscore her social station, Anne was brought up in the beautiful surroundings of Kensington Palace. For all of her social advantages, however, Anne's life was marred by misfortune and personal tragedy. From the age of twelve,[139] Anne was subject to head splitting migraines that would often confine her to bed for days at a time. The affliction, (now thought to be neurological), was accompanied by long bouts of exhaustion and deep sadness.[140] Throughout her long periods of agonizing convalescence, one of the great consolations of Anne's life remained her half-brother John. Something of their close bond and the intensity of Anne's illness is preserved in a letter from John composed in 1667:

> Dearest dear I must needs thinke life is but of a little extent, since mine is so embittered for your sake, that the world cannot make mee happy with all it can give mee unlesse I could render you so too. Ah my dear would I could put my selfe in a condition to be pittyd by my ennemies, if by it I could but provide you a perfect health, and would I could purchase it with any thing but the forfeiture of your love toward mee, so much I value thy dear affection, above all things else, and yet to make you happy I would part with that inestimable jewell, your kindnesse toward mee, though twere the bitterest temporal affliction.[141]

As their relationship attests, even in the depths of sickness, Anne never lost her delight in life and the deep comfort she gained from human sympathy. While extreme pain has a tendency of insulating the sufferer from the needs of others, in Anne's case it merely exaggerated her capacity for tenderness. In time, such affection would provide considerable relief when the world grew darker still. Soon after her marriage to the peer Edward Conway in 1651, Anne's physical suffering was swiftly compounded by gut-wrenching grief. She lost a two-year-old child to smallpox. These experiences left Anne with an intense preoccupation with the problem of evil. How could a God, loving, sublime and good, allow his creatures to endure pain and injury? What did these catastrophes mean in the context of eternity? Anne's answer to these thorny questions came in two interlocking forms, philosophical and confessional. As a young woman Anne had befriended John's university tutor, the Cambridge Platonist Henry More, (1614–1687). More had begun his philosophic voyage as a great admirer of the early experimental philosopher René Descartes, but eventually became a stern critic of the Cartesian separation of soul and matter. Freed from the spell of materialism, More proceeded to claim that far from being transcendent, divine energy was always at work in the emerging structure of the world. While always lesser than the Godhead, creation bore within itself the vital and unmistakable animation of divine purpose. As More expressed this divine indwelling: 'How indeed could He (God) communicate motion to matter,... if He did not touch the matter of the universe in practically the closest manner, or at least had not touched it at a certain time? Which certainly He would never be able to do if He were not present everywhere.'[142] God's radical intimacy with the world possessed profound theological implications for More. Firstly, God the creator was forever expressing his goodness in finite things. No sin nor outward destruction could obscure the life-giving activity of the Spirit. This led More to the position (expressed in a letter to Anne at the loss of her child)[143] that all things were under the right guidance of the divine life. In this identifiably Stoic posture, More thought we must accept all that comes to us as proper to the constitution of the universe. If all events stem from the operation of divine goodness, what does this tell us about the nature of created things? In resolving this question, More followed the venerable position of Plato in his dialogue *Timaeus*, that the whole universe was pervaded by a vital principle of conscious organization. The world was one body, suffused with a divine soul. Using this claim as a philosophical foundation, More proposed a form of Christian animism[144] in which all of nature was alive, interconnected, and capable of some degree of awareness. As Jasper Reid has summarised More's position:

> More had been committed to a doctrine of gradual monism whereby, since all things derived whatever reality they had from a God who had – or who was – the most perfect life, they themselves needed to possess some degree of life of their own, even if this might be tremendously attenuated

in terms of atoms, which by thickening and congealing together, would constitute gross bodies.[145]

Thus, for More, life was inherent in the cosmos, differing only in graduations of complexity. What did this commitment to ubiquitous animation mean for traditional accounts of salvation? More's sense of all-embracing divine presence led him to tentatively suppose that no one was excluded from the possibility of redemption. While by no means an advocate of Universal Salvation, More was convinced that the power of God would eventually overcome the force of sin that kept the world in subjection. As More expressed this hope in his *Divine Dialogues* 'sin at the long run shook hands with opacity. As much as the light exceeds the shadows, so much do the regions of happiness those of sin and misery'.[146] What did Conway do with More's decidedly holistic account of the cosmos? With a stunning capacity for integrating and synthesising complex ideas, Conway was adept at following More's argument and evaluating his philosophical sources. This exploration led her to adopt both More's commitment to divine intimacy and the spiritual animation of the cosmos. As Conway reflects in her posthumously published *The Principles of the Most Ancient and Modern Philosophy:*

> [There] is no Creature which does not receive something of his goodness, and this as much as possible and since the goodness of God is a living goodness, which possesses life, knowledge, love, and power, which he communicates to his creatures, how can it be, that any dead thing proceed from him, or be created by him, such as mere body or matter, according to their hypothesis, of those who affirm that matter cannot be changed into any degree of life or perception? It is truly said of one that God does not make death. It is equally true that he did not create any dead thing, for how can a

dead thing come from him who is infinite life and love?[147]

Despite following More in his Platonic animism to the letter, a close reading of Conway's treatise reveals that her philosophical work is not a straightforward facsimile of More's, but rather an attempt to filter his abstract philosophical categories through the prism of her own lived experience. In particular, Conway sought to develop a theological description of the world which was capable of relating the painful transience of existence with the abiding goodness of the God of Jesus Christ. It is here that the confessional sources of Conway's work come to the surface. In the early 1670s, at the urging of her Attender physician Francis Mercury van Helmont, Conway began to acquaint herself with the Quaker Way. In the course of her exploration, Conway corresponded with some of the leading lights of the early Quaker movement, including George Fox, Robert Barclay, George Keith[148] and William Penn. These encounters left an indelible mark upon Conway's religious and philosophical outlook. Firstly, she was awed by their radical acceptance of both hardship and stigma. As a strange and despised people, Quakers seemed to Conway perfect representatives of the simple, long-suffering Christianity practised by the Apostles. This impression was reinforced through the sober conduct of the Quaker serving women who worked in Anne's household. As Conway wrote to More in February 1675:

They have been and are a suffering people and are taught from the consolation [that] has been experimentally felt by them under their great tryals to administer comfort upon occasion to others in great distresse [...] the particular acquaintance with such living examples of great patience under sundry heavy exercises, both of bodily sicknesse andother calamitys (as some of them have related to me) I find begetts a more lively fayth and uninterrupted desire of approaching to such a behaviour in like exigencyes, then the most learned and Rhetorical discourses of resignation can doe.[149]

What was the significance of this moral example? For Anne this posture of quiet endurance was a means of maintaining her dignity in a world that had shrunk down to her bedroom walls. She needed no Church building or paid clergy to experience the restorative love of God, only the prayerful silence of pious women who could uphold her midst daily struggle. Something of this secluded prayer-life is preserved by a letter to Conway from the Quaker missionary Lilias Skene, who had visited Anne in the summer of 1677. Written shortly after her visit, Skene exhorts the bedridden Conway to attend to the example of Christ's cruciform suffering:

My desirs are that mor and mor that eye may be opened in thee that looks beyond the things that are seen, and in the living sence of the invisable glorie of the kingdom of god thou may live above the desir of temporarie satisfactions, craying secretly in thy heart that by all thy present suferings thin iniquetis may be perched away and senseteev netur be crusified, in the death of which shal com to regn whos right it is, and the conforter whom no man can tak from thee will dwel in thee and abyd with thee for ever.[150]

While such cruciate imagery was hardly novel in early Quaker texts, it took on an added resonance for a woman for whom physical extremity was a daily occurrence. Alongside this purgative account of misfortune, Conway found both philosophical and emotional comfort in the Quaker doctrine of the inward Light. It was More who had taught Conway that God was intimately bound up with his creation. Now under the garb of Fox's plain Christianity, the same truth was being restated. A universal Light dwelt in all, a candle of grace which accomplished God's saving work. Conway came to understand that Christ was more than a historical personality, but represented a vital conduit which connected all living beings together in their striving for God. In a seeming echo of Fox's own doctrine of Christ's presence even among unbelievers, Conway argues:

> Therefore, those who acknowledge such a mediator and believe in him can be said truly to believe in Jesus Christ, even though they do not yet know it and are not convinced that he has already come in the flesh. But if they first grant that there is a mediator, they will indubitably come to acknowledge also, even if they are unwilling, that Christ is the mediator.[151]

Thus, when Conway spoke and wrote to Friends, what she found was a kind of fulfilment of her earlier intellectual training. What More had laboured over with his mind, Friends had discovered with their hearts. What did this collision of More's philosophy and Quaker piety midst suffering produce? Perhaps the most stunning theological innovation concerned the question of Heaven and Hell. Rejecting the doctrine of eternal perdition, Conway lamented:

> For the common notion of God's justice, namely, that whatever the sin, it is punished with hellfire and without end, has generated a horrible idea of God in men, as if he was a cruel tyrant rather than an benign father towards all his creatures. If, however, an image of a lovable God were more widely known, such as he truly is, and shows himself in all his dealings with his creatures, and if our souls could inwardly feel and taste him, as he is charity and kindness itself, and as he reveals his intrinsic self through the light and spirit of our Lord Jesus Christ in the hearts of men, then, and only then, will men finally love him above everything and acknowledge as the most loving, just, merciful God, fit

to be worshipped before everything....[152]

Conway, who spent most of her life dependent on the compassion of others, could not conceive of the one she fled to in prayer as any less sympathetic than they. Empathy, not punishment, was the defining mark of Conway's theology. But if God is indeed pure love, how are we to explain the diverse calamities of mortal existence? To answer this question, Conway turned to More's Platonic animism. In a moment of beautiful lucidity, Conway suggests 'God has implanted a certain universal sympathy and mutual love into his creatures so that they are all members of one body'.[153] If all things are interconnected and inherently sympathetic, thought Conway, then the whole of creation is on the same journey of salvic fulfilment. Stones and minerals, plants and animals, are equal, equal, not in capacity, but in spiritual worth. This led Conway to accept a doctrine of cosmic transmigration as the means by which God saves the world from both sin and death. At the core of this account is a stunning reinterpretation of matter. Conway did not regard existent things as fixed entities, but rather considered each distinct thing as a centre of continuing transformation. Just as bodies transform 'food and drink ... [into] chyle and then into blood, and afterwards into spirits'[154] so all creatures are subject to radical transformations according to the inward state of their souls. Beings that grew in wisdom and self-understanding metamorphosed in ways that advanced their quest back to God, while those who stubbornly persisted in ignorance took forms intended to purify their souls of past obliviousness. As Conway notes:

[One] can infer that all God's creatures, which have previously fallen and degenerated from their original goodness, must be changed, and restored after a certain time to a condition which is not simply as good as that in which they were created, but better. The work of God cannot cease and thus it is the nature of every creature to be always in motion and changing from good to better and from good to evil or from evil back to good. And because it is not possible to proceed towards evil to infinity, since there is no example of infinite evil, every creature must turn again towards the good...[155]

This account of spiritual metamorphosis has ancient roots. Conway's theory closely echoed the thought of the ancient Neo-Platonist philosopher Plotinus, who had suggested that the cosmos was entirely one, but 'it is broken into unequal parts; hence the difference of place found in the Universe; better spots and worse; and hence the inequality of souls find their appropriate surroundings midst this local inequality'.[156] But despite these variations in goodness, it was Plotinus' contention that all things were on a slow advancement towards divine perfection. Affirming a Platonic doctrine of reincarnation, Plotinus regarded salvation, not as an event, but as a steady process of improvement. In the course of aeon-crossing transformations, suffering would arise, as a soul's errors and misperceptions were purged and corrected. This was Conway's theory also, that life after life, form after form, the divine image would be gradually restored in each creature. And since living beings had an eternity in which to rectify their shortcomings, all would return to perfection in the end. But if salvation is a universal inheritance, what is the role of Christ in this cosmic drama? It might be said that Conway's Christology consists of two parts, one related to creation, the other linked to the destiny of evolving souls. On the first theme, Conway tells us that '[When] Christ became flesh and entered into his body [...], he took on something of our nature and consequently of the nature of everything [...]. In assuming flesh and blood, he sanctified nature so that he could sanctify everything, just as it is the property of a ferment to ferment the whole mass'.[157]

There is a fascinating philosophical gesture here, evocative of the contemporary Protestant theologian Jürgen Moltmann. If Christ becomes one with all of nature through his Incarnation, then Christ stands in solidarity with the suffering of the cosmos. By sanctifying the created order, he makes the sorrows of the world a doorway to himself. As Conway reflects:

> [A]ll pain and suffering or torment stimulates the life or spirit existing in everything which suffers. As we see from constant experience and as reason teaches us, this must necessarily happen because through pain and suffering whatever grossness or crassness is contracted by the spirit or body is diminished; and so the spirit imprisoned in such grossness or crassness is set free and becomes more spiritual and, consequently, more active, and effective through pain.[158]

Doubtless in Anne's mind was Paul's image of salvation as a form of painful pregnancy, in which maternal birth pangs symbolise the liberation of all things (Romans 8:22–24). What does this analysis of creation mean for the progress of individual souls? For Conway, the notion of creation's purgative suffering signifies the utter determination of God to unite all spiritual persons, in whatever form they may be, to Godself. In the human world, this promise is made manifest in the two modes of Christ's coming. While the historical Christ appeared first in history, teaching perfection through his outward acts, he now manifests in the heart as the supreme rectifier of disturbed souls. As Conway describes this process through the language of therapeutic recovery:

> [In] his spiritual and inward appearance in men, he saves, heals, preserves, and restores their souls, and, as it were, subjects himself to suffering and death and for a certain period submits himself to the laws of time, that he might

elevate the souls of men above time, and corruption up to himself, in whom they receive blessing, and grow from one degree of goodness and virtue, and holiness forever.[159]

But what of those concrete social dimensions beyond the soul? What of the relationship between temporal Christian communities and eternity? For those seeking the Quaker underpinnings of Conway's philosophy, nothing is more immediately puzzling than her scant references to ecclesiastical life. Christ is identified by Conway under that ancient title of 'the husband and betrothed of the Church',[160] but Conway is manifestly uninterested in describing what the Church is and who might be properly expected to belong within it. There is some mention in Conway of perceived outsiders coming to believe in Christ, but this is not directly tied to any identifiable sect or parcel of Christendom. This lack of Church-language is strange given Conway's emerging Quaker sympathies. No matter how individualistic early Friends at first appeared, their inwardness and sense of separateness were always directed towards the building up of an imagined Church-life. Friends were not merely free agents of the Spirit, but a people gathered, who sought to gather others. The apparent reticence of Conway to ground her metaphysical excursions in a language of concrete community can be accounted for on the basis of three considerations. Firstly, we should be attentive to Conway's social and political context. Despite the relative peace and seclusion of Conway's life, the outside world had been riven by decades of civil and political strife which had culminated in the execution of Charles Stuart and the imposition of the Puritan Protectorate on a religiously fractured English Commonwealth. In such a world, the language of 'Church' had been the subject of dispute between competing sectarians and political authorities. Such an atmosphere was always liable to encourage some to disinvest themselves of the visible garb of 'Church' in a bid to strategically distance themselves from raging, and seemingly unresolvable, public conflicts. It was easy for Conway to sink into books and friendly correspondence, finding therein, an alternative way of approaching the religious collectivities of the outside world. Instead of approaching religious disputes hierarchically, through priests and bishops, Conway could approach these matters horizontally, through self-selected relationships of clustered seekers.

This tendency towards intimacy was much exaggerated by a second factor: the Platonic tradition that Conway had inherited from More. In both its ancient and early modern forms, Platonic philosophy depended upon an insular social imaginary which framed human experience in terms of individual and self-sufficient souls, hankering after what was perfect and beautiful. Plotinus had described the task of the Platonic disciple as 'the passing of solitary to solitary'.[161] Community, while never entirely irrelevant to the Platonic thinker, was nonetheless secondary to the life of ascetic contemplation that such spiritual journeying demanded. Combined with Conway's commitment to Quaker inwardness, it is easy to understand why the concept of the 'Church' might recede into the background. But religious belonging is not solely an intellectual exercise, but is always embodied and effective in character, embedded in particular practices, places, and sensations. When alterations occur in these sensual and spatial dimensions, religiosity changes form. This observation brings to our attention the third factor in Conway's seeming reluctance to use Church-talk, her repeated isolation from shared religious spaces. When illness progressively excludes people from the flow of collective social practice, alternative forms of group identification are needed to fill the gap. Imagined conversations, rooted in text, become a key way of sustaining social identity, while small-scale intimacies become more concrete than large-scale organizations. Older divisions between sacred and profane space collapse, causing religiosity to become unanchored from fixed social forms. The notion of 'Church' may still function as an imaginative or symbolic marker of belonging, but it is no longer tied to a localised mode of *Church-life*.

But we should not be deceived. Conway's lack of explicit ecclesiology does not signify an utterly privatised mode of self-focused religion. Indeed, what Conway lacks in Church-language, she more than makes up for with its holistic cosmology. For Conway, community lacks fixed markers not because creatures are self-contained mystical atoms, but because the entire universe, if seen from the perspective of Eternity, constitutes one great community brimming with life. If we consider this framework with a careful eye on the recurrent themes of interconnection and being-in-relation, we find that Conway's souls are never really alone, even if, for reasons of social necessity or philosophic practice, persons are sometimes isolated from large social groupings. In this way, contemplation does not mean abstraction, just as solitude does not imply aloofness. These two trajectories are illustrated through the interlocking assumptions of Conway's thought, namely the presence of myriad spiritual entities living alongside the natural and human worlds, combined with the assumption that life exists at all-levels of description, both on the macrocosmic and microcosmic planes of Being. At the level of the macrocosmic, Conway offers us glimpses of a universe filled with diverse angelic and infernal influences. When human beings walk through the world, each person is aided and advocated for by higher souls who desire human perfection. Echoing an ancient exegetical tradition,[162] Conway tells her reader that angelic ministering spirits accompany those humble of heart throughout their earthly lives (Matthew 18:10).[163] But according to Conway, the action of angels lies well beyond this traditional role of guardianship. When we read of angels in Scripture, Conway argues that we see potent illustrations of what we ourselves may one day become. As Conway expresses it 'a man who lives a pure and holy life on this earth, like the angels ... he is elevated to the rank of angels after he dies and becomes like them'.[164]

This formulation reveals two important facets of Conway's spirituality. Firstly, when viewed through Conway's overriding logic of sympathy, we can say that whoever lives out her highest goodness, belongs to the community of angels, no matter the outward conditions of life. No estrangement from public life nor religious ceremony changes this inward fact of belonging. Secondly, the case of the angels reveals to us that the spiritual world is always an encouragement to live out our best lives in the present. Heaven is an image of our progress, and not merely poetic solace or a spiritual afterthought. In the possibility of angelic ascent, we observe the true holism of Conway's philosophy. Eternity and temporality are not separate from one another, but merely scales of Being, which reflect one and the same world. The imperatives of Time are reflected in Eternity, just as the laws of Eternity are reflected in Time. But if this enfolding of eternity and temporality is illustrated by the angels, demonic entities are subject to the same moral laws of cause and effect. In Conway's seventeenth-century world, demonic forces were still a potent topic for discussion among clergymen and philosophers. In the popular imagination, demons were responsible not merely for misfortune, but inspired the diabolical activities of witches, warlocks, and heretics. Indeed, in the 1650s, Quakers frequently suffered from the accusation that they were demonic agents who spread godless beliefs among the gullible and misguided.[165] Conway makes few nods to these popular conceptions in her work, although she does not discount traditional pictures completely. She acknowledges that 'Christ struggles with evil spirits and the devil in the human heart'[166] and that these wretched beings inhabit landscapes of hellfire and punishment.[167] But given Conway's sense of the sheer oneness of Being, even the demons possess something of the divine light that propels all creatures on towards perfection. As Conway writes hopefully:

[I]t is therefore clear that no creature can become more and more a body to infinity, although it can become more and more a spirit to infinity. And nothing can become darker and darker to infinity, although it can become lighter and lighter to infinity. For this reason, nothing can be bad to infinity, although it can become better and better to infinity.[168]

There is something here of the third-century Christian exegete, Origen of Alexandria, (c. 184–c. 253), who entertained the possibility that at the end of time, even Satan and his fallen angels would be redeemed through the love of God.[169] Similarly for Conway, demons were not forever stigmatised Others, but creatures that had temporarily lost themselves to sin and ignorance. The dire situation of the demons differs from ours a little, to the extent that we are at another place on the same spiritual path. Our creaturely essence may presently enjoy somewhat superior conditions to these unclean spirits, but our soul-core is essentially the same as theirs. Indeed, we may yet come to experience the degraded position that the demons presently suffer, since all creatures can diminish or extend their capacities on the basis of their deeds. This establishes a strange kind of solidarity between the demons and humanity. Despite their pitiful condition, the devils are not consigned to their fate, for they, like us, will be reconciled with God in the fullness of time. While this expression of sympathetic redemption tells us much about Conway's vision of God, it also uncovers how the verities of the Eternal world should structure our daily existence. We are to forgive, to bear with, to hope and pity. There is no room in Conway's cosmology for either superiority or denunciation. We are to hold out for final restoration, as much for others as for ourselves. If the predicament of the demons is ultimately one of generous hope, it is these poor creatures, who assist Conway in understanding the way Life and Mind are suffused throughout the cosmos. Reflecting on the exorcism of the Gerasene demons in the Synoptic Gospels, Conway notes:

> [Just] as a spirit of brute or man, is nothing but a countless multitude of bodies collected into one and arranged into a certain order, so the spirit of man or brute is also a countless multitude of spirits united in a single body.... Just as the devil, who assaulted the man was called Legion because there were many of them. Thus, every human being, indeed every creature whatsoever contains many spirits and bodies.[170]

Underlying this novel theory of a plurality of bodies and souls within the seeming fixity of matter, is Conway's acute sense of the sheer grandeur of God. Complaining of those materialists who claims that 'the number of creatures is finite', Conway calls the God they worship 'an idol of their own imagination whom they confine to narrow space'.[171] In place of a quantifiable and circumscribed world, Conway argues that the microcosm consists of *worlds within worlds* and lives within lives. Conway suggests that 'an infinite number of creatures can be contained and exist inside the smallest creatures and that all these could be bodies and in their own way mutually impenetrable'.[172] This is an exhilarating notion, for it makes the world a true mirror of the incalculable depths of God. For Conway, the more the mind dug into the depths of things, the more wonders it would discover, vitality within vitality, and organization within organization. While much of Conway's daily experience was confined to her bed chamber, she felt herself to be a joyful a point of habitation, for creatures brimming with creatures that were themselves connected to the ever-present love of God.

What should we make of Conway's philosophical endeavour and her attempts to place it within the stream of Quaker spirituality? When George Fox detected the influence of Conway's philosophy within local Meetings (through Friends closely identified with Conway's physician, Francis Mercury van Helmont[173]), he was scandalised. Fox did not dispute the grandeur of Conway's hope for the restoration of all creation, nor her spiritual sincerity, but he questioned the sources upon which such hope was based. With their commitment to the transfiguration of souls, the universal animation of nature, and a suspicious interest in Cabala, Helmontian Friends appeared to be diverting Quaker faith from the pure wellsprings of primitive Christianity which many early Quaker preachers, including Fox, espoused.[174] The open-ended conjecture of Anne and her circle, seemed to have little to do with the plain and earthy testimony of Scripture, which was an aid, not to the haughty and learned, but to the humble and pure in heart. Fox's impatience may anticipate an equal exasperation among many contemporary Liberal Quakers, whose scorn of theologising, constitutes something of a shared dogma. And there is both truth and wisdom in the exasperation, particularly in this case. It is true that when we encounter Conway's Quaker Way, we are forced to confront a grand system, as complex and abstract as the theological monoliths of the Christian past, those grand projects of Gregory of Nyssa, of Maximus the Confessor, and Augustine of Hippo. In surveying these cathedrals of ingenuity, we might ask: What has the Academy of Plato, or the speculation of metaphysicians, got to do with the unadorned walls of the Meeting House? But in taking an inflexible stance against philosophical systems per se, we are in danger of assuming that all methodical attempts at stating the essence of faith are hollow replicas of the living fountain. Such a judgement forgets the role of the heart in the production of such schemes, and their genuine desire to communicate what is vital and true in the builders' experience. In the case of Anne Conway, her philosophy stemmed from a prior intuition of God, which she sought to understand through the tools of the mind. As Conway tells us:

> For God is infinitely good, loving, and bountiful; indeed, he is goodness and charity itself, the infinite fountain and ocean of goodness, charity, and bounty. In what way is it possible for that fountain not to flow perpetually and to send forth living waters? For will not that ocean overflow in its perpetual emanation and continual flux for the production of creatures? For the goodness of God is communicated and multiplied by its own nature, since in himself he lacks nothing, nor can anything be added to him because of his absolute fullness and his remarkable and mighty abundance.[175]

True, such God-language can easily fall into a lifeless and stifling 'ism', but this is not true in Conway's case. A God of relentless vitality and love was the real object of her life, not mere philosophising for its own sake. What she wrote and thought was a mere leaky boat to carry her to the shores of a deeper faith. In this way, we might say that Conway's system is an example of the rational mind writing a love letter to God. In this task, Conway brought all she was, her passion, her sympathy, and crucially, her illness. She sought to find words big enough to encompass and affirm her pain and distress. She refused to accept that God abandons sufferers, that even in conditions of unspeakable anguish, God is still working for the happiness of his creatures. Conway stood on the shoulders of philosophy to make sense of the heavy burdens of life and, in so doing, cleared the way for a deeper prayer and piety. She desired the cessation of intellectual doubt so that her heart could better serve the imperatives of truth. Looked at in this way, Conway's system is not a dead husk that stands in the way of genuine experience, but the intense crystallisation of spiritual biography, framed as propositions and axioms. No matter how speculative, Conway's project is an exposition of the Gospel, an expression of its universality and its faithfulness towards the lost, albeit framed in the metaphysics of early modern philosophy. This does not lessen its power, or the degree to which it is a description of Christ's cosmic story. We may disagree with it in parts, we may be bewildered by it to some degree, but if we sink under the surface of its concepts, we find hope, regeneration, and healing.

Anne Conway and the Enchanted World

At this juncture, it may be justly asked: Of what use is a seventeenth-century philosophy of God and nature to contemporary Friends? Given this chapter's discussion of animism, angels, and demons, the reader can be forgiven for thinking that the present writer has departed from the realms of reality and dived headlong into the murky terrain of baffling fantasy. This is a common reaction, even among otherwise spiritual Friends. In his 2013 Swarthmore Lecture, Gerald Hewitson observed that 'we tend to dismiss as superstitious, childish, or uneducated, any talk of the devil, demons, or spirits'.[176] Then what should we moderns do with early Quaker descriptions of paranormal evil and disembodied goodness? The answer, suggests Hewitson, lies in a proper appreciation of the acute mental realities of sin and redemption which sit behind otherwise bizarre descriptions of devilish darkness and angelic light. Instead of treating spiritual visitations as moments of external supernatural contact, Hewitson suggests instead, that we interpret these images as potent symbols of internal moral conflict. Turning to the personified language of evil in the preaching of George Fox, Hewitson suggests: 'If, for a moment, instead of seventeenth-century language, we translate "talk of spirits and demons" through the prism of twenty-first-century psychological insight'[177] we will come to a correct appreciation of the complex 'human condition'[178] which early

145

Friends sought to express. There is, I think, merit in Hewitson's interpretative proposal, especially when coupled with the language of 'temptation' and 'sin'. Early Friends certainly were wrestling with psychological fixations and private hells to which they applied a highly personalised language of spiritual agency. But in holding too keenly to this psychological reading of early Friends' experience, we end by taming our religious language in ways that simply underwrite secular assumptions about the nature of the world.

If angels and demons are mere figments of internal psychological processes, why should God be treated any differently? After all, our modern psychological approach to spiritual phenomena tends to assume that religious experiences are confined to our heads and do not relate to anything 'really out there' in the world. This is as true of the agnostic psychology of William James as it is of the highly spiritual psychological method of C.G. Jung. In this account, 'psychic facts' may possess a kind of weight or objectivity within, but they have no purchase, or analogue in the external realm of 'hard facts'. Our stories might be meaningful to us, but this meaning is never found outside ourselves. What this psychological approach misses is the unsettling possibility that some people really do have genuine experiences of spiritual realms 'outside' their minds. Unmined in the modern division between 'hard' and 'soft' facts, is the possibility that there are spiritual entities, (God, angels, spirits), who work both within us and outside us. This is an inescapable feature of early Quakerism, which moderns, especially Liberal mystics, are eager to domesticate. In place of a *buffeted self* that regards itself as a meaning-maker in an otherwise meaningless world, early Friends assumed the existence of a *porous self* that lived in an 'enchanted' cosmos. Charles Taylor, in his masterful study *A Secular Age,* has defined enchantment in the following terms:

[The] boundary between agents and forces is fuzzy in the enchanted world; and the boundary between mind and world is porous ... The porousness of the boundary emerges here in the various kinds of "possession", all the way from a full taking over of the person, as with a medium, to various kinds of domination by, or partial fusion with, a spirit or God. Here ... the boundary between self and other is fuzzy, porous. And this has to be seen as a fact of *experience,* not a matter of "theory", or "belief.[179]

The last point is crucial. In the present epoch, it is easy to flatten Taylor's description into a series of propositional beliefs (as a series of concepts), when in fact, enchantment constitutes the prioritising of particular sensations like awe, affirmation, synchroneity, and symbolic significance, as decisive states that uncover *life's true colours.* The enchanted person looks for signs, messages, and purposes in the flow of experience. Enchanted perception assumes that meaning is there *to be found,* and not merely made. Instead of viewing life as a series of accidents, enchanted people labour to appreciate the interconnection between events and thoughts, interior intuitions, and outward happenings. In the enchanted world, emotions, beliefs, and intentions have an external weight, in the transfer of blessing or the potency of prayer. Things of the Spirit can suffuse what seems solid, separate, or impossibly distant. Unlike the secular account, the mind can 'travel'. Thoughts or desires are able to touch what seems past, (perhaps the dead) or even the future, (the envisioning of worlds or events yet to come). Taken together, we should think of enchantment, less as a position and more a lens through which life is interpreted and understood. While the enchanted person is acutely mindful of intense experiences of indwelling meaning, a secular person regards any intuition of extra-human significance as ambiguous, insubstantial, and ultimately peripheral. A modern secular person may very well experience brief intuitions of a more enchanted world, through art, music, or poetry, but these experiences are infrequent and truncated. These 'thin' enchantments have no community to sustain them, nor a stable set of symbols to describe them. They constitute flashes of the sacred, not a framework for sacred living.

How do these distinctions help us understand the significance of Conway's work? If we place Conway beside Taylor's account, we find that her philosophical approach straddles the developing divide between enchantment and secularity. A key problem for Conway is why modern philosophy has broken away from the vision of cosmic sympathy that underlies her work. For Conway, nothing concrete has changed in the world that would account for the nascent secular view of life, but something has altered in the minds of philosophic inquirers. The elites of the seventeenth century, to use Kelly's observation, had begun to treat this-sidedness as possessing greater weight than Eternity. They began to view articulations of Heaven, (especially as embodied in popular beliefs and practices) as vain superstitions which reduce the value and scope of earthly life. This view was already present in the likes of Machiavelli, but it found its most coherent expression during the emergence of mechanical science. This shift was not in itself atheistic, although the new focus on 'the world' had the effect of drawing philosophy away from older tasks, among them establishing the link between things of time and things of eternity. In this new cosmology of control and outcome, philosophical projects were increasingly measured by practical and empirical yardsticks, not according to ultimate realities. In the dialogue *Timaeus,* Plato had defined creation as a moving image of eternity, but under the new science, the world was viewed as a series of quantities to catalogue, dissect, and manipulate. Disputing these moves in Benedict Spinoza and Thomas Hobbes, Conway suggested that their experimental philosophy reduced the world to a largely lifeless mechanism, a cosmic clock,[180] whose motions operated independently of any indwelling divine activity. Insofar as God remained part of these new systems, Godself became something like a natural object, 'nothing more than a body'[181] (Hobbes) or else a name for the totality of creatures[182] (Spinoza). To these materialistic theologies, Conway replies that these constructions do untold damage 'to the human race, to true piety and in contempt of the most glorious name of God'.[183] What lies behind these strong words? Taylor, in an illuminating discussion of pre-modern morality, gets to the heart of the matter, when he suggests that the kind of Platonic picture adopted by the likes of Conway assumes both the inherent goodness and perfectibility of the world. In such a scheme, morality is not a mere human convention, but something which is woven into the very structure of Being itself. In this account, the cosmos

> sets the paradigm purposes for the beings within it. As humans we are to conform to our Idea, and this in turn must play its part in the whole, which among other things involves our being "rational", i.e., capable of seeing the self-manifesting order. No one can understand this order while being indifferent to it or failing to recognize its normative force... The move to mechanism neutralizes this whole domain. It no longer sets norms for us or defines crucial life meanings.[184]

To turn the universe into a finite mechanism, or a terrain devoid of spirit, dissolves any sense that the world is 'for' anything. Thus, we see that the issue of how we treat Fox and Conway's language of 'spirits' is more than a matter of believing in this or that entity. How we treat intimations of the demonic or angelic exposes in turn how we treat Eternity. Are the depths of Divine Life a vital source of meaning and action for us, or like the secular world at large, do we confine the timelessness at the heart of time to our heads? Does goodness *really* pervade the depths of things or is the experience of ultimate goodness the result of overactive human brains? Do we trust our stories when they speak of a deeper domain of Being, or are we content to psychologise them? It is this dilemma between porous enchantment and interiorised secularity that constitutes the essence of Conway's thought. Having decried a world of soulless materialism, Conway reflects: '[Without] taking refuge in some forced metaphor, we can understand the words of Christ, that "God can raise up children to Abraham from stones" (Matthew 3:9). And if anyone should deny the omnipotence of God ... to raise up the sons of Abraham from external stones, this surely would be a great presumption.'[185] One may find this final appeal to *believe in the unbelievable* an accurate summation of Conway's Quaker philosophy. But consider these sentences in terms of an orientation towards life. Do we believe death is an absolute? Or will life prevail over decay? Is there a Love and Power that will transform all things? Or is the world marching towards a slow disintegration? Is the battle for justice and beauty ultimately futile? Or will these things be upheld in Eternity? These questions are not as abstract as they first appear, since they go to the heart of how we live in the world. If there are the kinds of depths Conway and Fox proclaim, then both life and death subsist within a larger story of creation, journey, and renewal. If these realities live in us, aren't we obliged to make different choices from those who regard the world as all there is? Aren't we urged to hope and love when others have given up on both? In the final part of this chapter, I attempt to firm up these intuitions by considering the ethical dimensions of the arguments just sketched. As I go on to show, Conway's interpretation of the Quaker Way implies the practical task of creating a durable community of sympathy, one which is inspired by the unity of all life. At the centre of this cosmic ethic is the perpetual expansion of compassion, a mode of co-suffering and co-caring which encompasses both heaven and earth. While this model of Quaker community seems impossibly grand to embody, I argue that Conway's steadfast faith in simple acts of kindness is the beginning of this majestic path. In every life rescued, in every person affirmed, in every suffering acknowledged and held, we become part of a larger world, which transcends place and time.

Compassion and the Life of Heaven

We shall not cease from exploration/And the end of all our exploring/Will be to arrive where we started/And know the place for the first time. (T.S. Eliot)

The concept of cosmic restoration is an old one among Christians. Early in the Acts of the Apostles, Peter proclaims: 'Heaven must receive him [Christ] until the time comes for God to restore everything, as he promised long ago through his holy prophets' (Acts 3:21). But how was everything to be restored? One of the most majestic and controversial meditations on this theme of restoration was provided by Origen of Alexandria. In the third book of his treatise, *On First Principles*, Origen suggests that the restoration of the world will come about through the slow transformation of pre-existent human souls, who, after their earthly deaths, will continue to progress spiritually through countless worlds and ages. As Origen notes:

This, then, is how we must suppose that events happen in the consummation and restitution of all things, namely, that souls, advancing and ascending little by little in due measure and order, first attain to that other earth and the instruction that is in it, and are there prepared for those precepts to which nothing can ever be added.[186]

In this way, Origen imagined the cosmos as a kind of divine

school, in which the precepts of Christ will be taught to each, needful soul, tailored to their circumstances. Central to Origen's educative understanding of restoration was a gradualist account of moral perfection. Instead of a static cosmos of permanent essences consigned either to eternal perdition or perpetual bliss, Origen tells us that 'God can transform and transfer' bodies 'into any form or species he desires as the merits of things demand.'[187] The innate plasticity of created things ensures the 'improvement and correction' of finite creatures through 'infinite and immeasurable ages'.[188] On the surface, this exposition of salvation places Conway firmly within Origen's thought-world. Indeed, as Conway's biographer Sarah Hutton has argued: 'As far as she can be said to be an Origenist in spirit, Anne Conway was, arguably, a more thorough-going Origenist than Henry More, who did not subscribe to Origen's doctrine of universal salvation or his denial of the eternity of hell.'[189] Certainly, Conway joins Origen in envisioning redemption as the gradual and universal improvement of souls through a series of aeon-crossing transformations. Both affirm a Platonic cosmology which assumes a hierarchical and perfectible universe. But these notable overlaps should not disguise substantial theological differences. While Origen's account of salvation is recognizably universal, it does not anticipate Conway's doctrine of universal transformation, particularly her willingness to place immortal souls into non-human animals.[190] While conceding that non-human animals possess spirits after a fashion, Origen denies that these are the same as eternal human souls.[191] Moreover, while Origen claimed that all creatures benefit from the blessing of God, non-human animals only do this as secondary beneficiaries of the supreme gifts God bestows first to human beings.[192] Conway certainly follows doctrinal convention when she notes that 'the earth gave human beings the best and most excellent spirits' insofar as human souls are ordained to dominate lesser terrestrial spirits.[193] But such anthropocentrism is never held consistently by Conway, who repeatedly emphasises the abiding love of God for all souls in whatever creature they reside. It may be thought that these distinctions are little more than speculative quibbles. But this is not so. They point to the kind of life Conway believes she can live in the eye of Eternity, an ethic characterised by boundary-crossing care. While Origen desires to tell a more or less human salvation-story, Conway wants something arguably grander, a mind and heart open towards all beings. We find evidence of this generous attitude in Conway's discussion of the intrinsic sympathy between all created things. As Conway suggests:

> God endowed man with the same instinct for justice towards beasts and the trees of the field. For any man who is just and good loves the brute creatures which serves him, and he takes care of them, so that they have food and rest and the other things they need. He does not do this only for his own good but out of a principle of true justice; and if he is so cruel towards them that he requires work from them and nevertheless does not provide the necessary food, then he has surely broken the law which God inscribed in his heart. And if he kills any of his beasts to satisfy his own pleasure, he acts unjustly, and the same measure will be measured out to him.[194]

This passage contains several moral commitments worthy of note. Firstly, there is an implied duty of compassion of human beings towards plants. Secondly, there is an implied denunciation of blood sports, (a topic that much exercised early Quaker moralists[195]), and thirdly, there is the suggestion that those who torment other beings will be tormented in turn. Clustered together, these commitments tell us much about Conway's conception of Eternity. For Conway, living in the presence of Eternity means first and foremost the cultivation of radical compassion. There is no angelic life for us without attending to those souls who journey alongside us in myriad different forms. When it comes to non-human animals, thinks Conway, our care should not emerge from an arrogant sense of largess, but because 'God has implanted a certain universal sympathy and mutual love into his creatures so that they are all members of one body and all, so to speak, brothers, for whom there is one Father'.[196] Given Conway's sense that our moral concern should be as ubiquitous as the entities that we encounter, a rich vein of resemblance may be drawn between her Platonic ethics of mutual love and the high-minded morality of the scientist and theologian Albert Schweitzer. In his 1923 study *Civilization and Ethics*, Schweitzer defines the kernel of morality as 'reverence for life'. Schweitzer concedes that as a species of self-reflective beings, humans are caught in something of a moral bind. We are aware that we must take and consume life in order to live. As Schweitzer expresses this painful contradiction: 'The world is a ghastly drama of the-will-to-live divided against itself. One existence makes its way at the cost of another; one destroys the other.'[197] While this might encourage us towards a position of paralysing guilt, Schweitzer suggests another course, the practice of repeated sympathy at every possible opportunity. This emerges out of a sense, ever present in Conway that 'the will-to-live has come to know about other-wills-to-live. There is in it a yearning to arrive at unity, to become universal'.[198] It is this lofty conception of observing life as a whole that permits Schweitzer to stray close to Conway's animism, noting approvingly that 'in and behind all phenomena there is the-will-to-live'.[199] While neither give us ethical direction about how to care for a river or a mountain, we can say that both Schweitzer and Conway cultivate the same orientation towards existence, an abundance of sympathy, a joy in life, the avoidance of cruelty, and the cultivation of an expansive sense of care. As Schweitzer expresses this ethic:

A man is truly ethical only when he obeys the compulsion to help all life which he is able to assist and shrinks from injuring anything that lives. He does not ask how far this or that life deserves one's sympathy as being valuable, nor beyond that, whether and to what degree it is capable of feeling. Life as such is sacred to him…. If he walks on the road after a shower and sees an earthworm which has strayed on to it, he bethinks himself that it must get dried up in the sun, if it does not return soon enough to the ground in which it can burrow, so he lifts it from the deadly stone surface and puts it on the grass. If he comes across an insect which has fallen into a puddle, he stops a moment in order to hold out a leaf or a stalk on which it can save itself.[200]

For Schweitzer and Conway, such actions are always animated by the sense of 'the will-to-live, stirring everywhere'.[201] But what of ultimate things? In a world of such obvious suffering and struggle, what is a reverence for life aiming at? It is here that Schweitzer and Conway most decidedly part company. For all Schweitzer's appeal to what he calls, a 'mysticism of the ethical union of Being',[202] his commitment to life's sanctity is not framed by any theological depth. Schweitzer delights in oceanic feelings of oneness, but these sensations remain avowedly poetic and resolutely non-metaphysical. Indeed, as Schweitzer reassures an assumedly secular reader: '[This ethic] … need give no answer to the question of what significance the ethical man's work for the maintenance, promotion, and enhancement of life can be in the total happenings of nature.'[203] For Conway such a view of life is fundamentally deficient. It is not simply that we are alive and so, in a kind of rarefied narcissism, should love all that lives. We should love the created world, because it is a manifestation of the Eternal depths that unfailingly delights in all that lives. In this scheme, compassion is not merely a vehicle for moving closer to other lives, it is the means of enriching and enacting Eternity. If every refined soul becomes an angelic being, then every act of care extends, little by little, the boundaries of Heaven. In such an ethic, we aid in the repair of a creation that is straining for release and unity, true, but this moral project is not about us; it is about the God *who loves us*. Whether we succeed in revering life as we ought, the Life that is in us is destined for the ungraspable grace of final unity. It is because of God's Eternity that failures will eventually blossom into victories and our crushing evils will eventually fall away, having become sublime goodness, light as a feather and as soft as wool. This does not mean that our walk along this cosmic road does not matter, or that all directions are, come what may, equal. Conway's Universalism is not a creed of resignation or apathy. To affirm the long journey of the soul is to accept the wide expanse of responsibility. In the course of a fascinating interpretation of the destruction of Sodom (Genesis 19), Conway notes:

> [The] sins of this world, like the sins of Sodom, which had to be destroyed by fire, appear to be more like the sins of the devil than anything else because of their hostility, malice, cruelty, fraud, cunning. Therefore their appropriate punishment is fire, which is the original essence of those so noble yet degenerate, spirits, and by this same fire they must be degraded and restored.[204]

Conway is clear that evil is a canker that causes souls to scorch and wound themselves. The more such spirits hang back on the road, forgetting themselves in hatred and cruelty, the greater the force needed to correct them. Our choices have weight in the scheme of the world, since they determine the character of our journey, whether it will be smooth or rough, delayed, or direct. But for all the dignity Conway affords to free will, her philosophy resists any suggestion that the individual self is all, or that, in some sense, the world depends upon us. Conway inoculates us from such self-involvement by bidding us to consider the final goal of all things. When we love truly and care deeply, we do indeed hasten a cosmic process of perfection, but even when we fall back, our place in the Home of God is never in doubt. Conway's theology is no crude commendation of 'works' but rather a meditation on the cosmic activity of God. Heaven is where we are always meant to be, not as a prize we have earnt, but because we are marked by the goodness of our Creator. And since goodness sings to goodness, the stream will carry us to the bank sooner or later. As 2 Timothy reminds us, 'our Saviour ... wants everyone to be saved and to come to the knowledge of the truth' (2:3–4). And what God desires, God will accomplish. Consequently, we should live our lives, not in endless worry, but with the confidence that our small acts, whether they succeed or fail, will make ripples in the deep waters of Heaven. Conway's generous attitude to life and Eternity goes right to the heart of so much contemporary reflection on the meaning of 'Testimony', and the difference between distinctly Quaker actions and open-handed humanitarianism. Too often in Friends, we are eager to adopt the political imperatives of the world, without first articulating our Quaker story's deepest convictions. Jesus' words about worldly wealth could easily be applied to the seductive cult of political activity divorced from spiritual hope:

> Do not store up for yourselves treasures on earth, where moths and vermin destroy, and where thieves break in and steal. But store up for yourselves treasures in heaven, where moths and vermin do not destroy, and where thieves do not break in and steal. For where your treasure is, there your heart will be also. (Matthew 6: 19)

What then are our Quaker treasures? Our greatest gem is our rebellious hope. Quakers work in the world, not solely to make the machine of civilization run more smoothly, but because we desire to communicate something of the Life and Power which nourishes our vision and kindles our faith. We seek to make the Kingdom of God real to a world that has no room for the tender presence of angels, but listens far too readily to the despair of the demons. But we can only live according to such hope if we first discard the pretention of being socially useful. Once we have disinvested ourselves of the glittering jewels of relevance, we can finally be free to fail by the standards of our secular age, and prosper by the lights of Heaven. Our present epoch is obsessed with 'knowing the right thing to do', 'having a plan', 'being good and being seen to be good'. This is not the primary focus of our Quaker Way. We believe in goodness, but we do not believe that goodness is achieved merely through ceaseless activity. We need to go deeper than our contemporary world will allow. Eternity teaches us that no action is wasted, and no wrong turn is irreversible. If we wish to do good, we must first learn to forgive, to recognise ourselves in others, and come to understand that we all walk the same road. As Schweitzer expressed the task so well:

> All acts of forbearance and of pardon are for them acts forced from one by sincerity towards oneself. I must practise unlimited forgiveness because, if I did not, I should be wanting in sincerity to myself, for it would be acting as if I myself were not guilty in the same way as the other has been guilty towards me. Because my life is so liberally spotted with falsehood, I must forgive falsehood which has been practised upon me; because I myself have been in so many cases wanting in love, and guilty of hatred, slander, deceit, or arrogance, I must pardon any want of love, and all hatred, slander, deceit, or arrogance which have been directed against myself. I must forgive quietly and unostentatiously.[205]

Nowhere is this vision more powerfully illustrated than in

Conway's affirmation of the final redemption of the demons. Their lives, hardened and distant from God, are reflections of our own cold hearts. If we can imagine a greater life for them in the heart of God, surely we can forgive both ourselves and others? At the core of this conception is the image of the Cross, and its majestic conception of saving love. The cruciform life redeems, not by power, but by giving over, by tender concern, and co-suffering. It judges what is right, not according to utility or acclamation, but according to whether an act has made space for God's joy in the world. This ethic of mutual healing is quite different from the modern ethos of effectiveness. Here, the primary goal of life is not to build or reform, but rather to love and cherish, and then let God do the rest. Instead of worrying about whether *we are making a difference*, we can root down into the deep virtues of our Quaker Way, not success, but hopefulness, not achievement, but humility, not outcomes, but faithfulness. When we sit together in Worship, we are not gathered to be good, to be active, to be valuable, but to remind the world that there is a Spirit and a Light greater than states and armies, greater than parties and programmes, even greater than planetary survival. It is the hope that lives when all our plans come to nothing, when we feel abandoned by the future. As Paul expressed it: 'For I am convinced that neither death nor life, neither angels nor principalities, neither the present nor the future, nor any powers, neither height nor depth, nor anything else in all creation, will be able to separate us from the love of God that is in Christ Jesus our Lord' (Romans NIV 8: 38–9).

Conclusion

What Is Tradition?

> Once we were safe on shore, we learned that we were on the island of Malta. The people of the island were very kind to us. It was cold and rainy, so they built a fire on the shore to welcome us ... we were showered with honours, and when the time came to sail, people supplied us with everything we would need for the trip. (Acts 28)

As I pen the final pages of this book, I am conscious that my argument, at times highly critical of Liberal Quakerism, may be in fact a contribution to the very Liberal tradition it seeks to critique. After all, this book has not argued for theological purity, or the resumption of some exact standard of Quaker morality. Certainly, I have returned to the past for resources, but not all aspects of the Quaker story have been given equal weight in my search. For instance, no defence has been made of traditional Quaker speech, or 'plain dress'. I have not suggested that Elders direct their attention to the moral monitoring of Friends beyond the Meeting House door, and not chastise wayward members who 'marry out'. Astute readers may well find these absences illuminating. They suggest that whatever my reservations, I am still a Liberal Quaker, albeit one who refuses to jettison the depths of the Christian imagination in the name of some bland, generic 'spirituality'. I find I do not want Quakerism to be 'pure', but I do want it to be rich, substantial, and whole. My account of Quaker repair is 'traditionalist' in the limited sense that I regard tradition (the cumulative insights of the Quaker Way) as something worth cherishing. But like all bodies of knowledge, Quaker wisdom is a living, breathing, contested reality. It is not an orderly little object in a museum display case, but something loved, embraced, and lived through. It is closer to a forest than a book, closer to a roaring river than a stable mountain. Such embodied knowledge needs to be sifted, wrestled with, navigated, walked in, and criticised. As the moral philosopher Alasdair MacIntyre once observed 'when a tradition is in good order it is always partially constituted by an argument about the goods the pursuit of which gives to that tradition its particular point and purpose... Traditions, when vital, embody continuities of conflict'.[206] Understood in these active terms, tradition is not some arbitrary dead weight on our freedom, but the expression of a creative tension, the contours of which give our actions their shared context and direction. This cultural background is knit together with our thoughts and words, sometimes loving, sometimes bad-tempered, but always adding to a definite whole. The Quaker worldview is not simple or tidy, but it is life-giving for those who inhabit it.

This leads us to a central aspect of tradition's inner nature. When we truly occupy a shared culture, we are encouraged to add to a conversation across time, in which we come back again and again to the meaning of our tradition. In this way, a Quaker return to the depth of the Christian narrative is not an invitation to embrace some inauthentic faith of historical re-enactment, but instead begin again the vital task of sustaining an energetic dialogue about who we are. To refuse roots in the name of individual spirituality not merely abdicates responsibility for the creative dialogue that tradition requires, it fundamentally endangers authentic spirituality. It places on the shoulders of the individual the intolerable burdens of 'working it all out' for himself. It leaves the spiritual voyager alone, precisely at those moments when mutual care and collective seeking is most sorely needed. But in claiming that individual Quakers are best served by a collective spiritual storehouse, I do not wish to suggest that Friendly Wisdom is somehow walled off from the wider streams of the world – from other sacred traditions, from art, from literature, from science and from philosophy. Wisdom is wisdom wherever it is found. Liberal Quakerism has always been right to emphasise this fact, not because this posture is 'liberal', but because it is Quaker. To say that truth has no walls is not some post-modern addition to our Quaker story. To the contrary, it is woven into the fundamental grammar of how Quakers have always spoken about God, the Spirit, and the ministry of Christ. Returning to our deep roots does not negate the Liberal love of diversity but enlarges it. Under the tender wings of the Universal Christ, we can deepen our commitment to loving multiplicity, without forsaking substantial shared theological claims. In this vein, I have suggested that Liberal Quakers should embrace diversity not because we fear to say definite things about the life of the Spirit, but because we can speak confidently about the Light that unfailingly nourishes us. My plea is not for doctrinal conformity, but for a symbolic centre around which we can gather and be known for who we really are. Among the ancient Greeks, this notion of a spiritual centre was beautifully exemplified by the practice of *xenia*, welcome towards strangers. It was the custom, not merely to feed and clothe lonely foreigners wronged on the road, but to offer the profoundest of salves, the safety for the stranger to put words around *their story*. In a particularly moving scene from Book 8 of Homer's *Odyssey*, we see the shipwrecked hero, Odysseus, stand before King Alcinous, gushing tears. Instead of turning away this battered stranger, the king asks his weary guest:

Tell me the name by which you were known at home to your mother and father and friends in the town and country round. No one, after all, whether of low or high degree, goes nameless once he has come into the world; everybody is named by his parents when he is born. You must also tell me where you come from, to what people and to what city you belong so that my sentient ships may plan the right course to convey you there... And now, speak and tell us truly, where have you been driven in your wanderings? What parts of the inhabited world have you visited? (8:547–574)[207]

The bloodstained world of Homer possessed few absolutes and even fewer rights, but even in the midst of war and the relentless expansion of city walls, the narrative dignity of each appeared an indisputable fact. There is no comprehensive resurrection in Homer, no grand *eschaton*, but there is the dignity granted to a life which is capable of being told and remembered. Odysseus, reduced to a tattered beggar, is thought to deserve a fire where he can be called by name and recall himself to others. By pondering things lost to time, (old loyalties, affections, and extended ties of memory) Odysseus re-enters the human world. This is the deep medicine of tradition. When we have a place to stand, we can finally name and recall both ourselves and others. At its finest, a shared story represents the fracturing of painful solitude into beloved community, where we know and are known. As God says in Scripture: 'Do not fear, for I have redeemed you; I have summoned you by name; you are mine' (NIV Isaiah 43:1). While each person undoubtedly has a unique path to walk, in the tender embrace of the Quaker story, we always have a place to return. We may travel far within our own souls, through spiritual forests and wildernesses, past citadels, and towers of great insight. But wherever we roam, there is a place we can be looked for and grounded. Such a grand conception of tradition needs neither fundamentalism nor dogmatism to bolster it. Its structure is sustained, not by fear of the outside world or the heavy yoke of internal discipline, but by a joyful confidence in its own highest hopes. In the accent of Quaker Christianity, this is the hope that all creatures, all pasts, and all futures, find their fulfilment in the love of God. As T.S. Eliot expressed this mystical truth in *The Four Quartets*:

Footfalls echo in the memory
Down the passage which we did not take
Towards the door we never opened
Into the rose-garden.
Time present and time past
Are both perhaps present in time future
And time future contained in time past.
What might have been and what has been
Point to one end, which is always present.[208]

The sense that time ushers us towards timelessness should lead us to the following posture as Friends. The Quaker Meeting House is neither flower nor sunlight. It possesses no fountains nor green grasses of its own. It is only a portal to God's garden. Quaker tradition (like all living tradition) does not exist for itself, but for the sake of the beauty which stirs it. Quakerism rises and falls on the basis of where it leads to. No authentic Quakerism leads back to itself. Tradition is a servant, not a master. I hope this latter explanation goes some way towards blunting those parts of the book which some Friends found prickly, confrontational, or uncomfortable. Where I have offered critique of certain threads in contemporary Quaker Liberalism, my intention was not to question the spiritual depth, intellectual rigour, or integrity of Friends with whom I disagreed. Rather, I have attempted to express a richer vision of Quaker Christianity than many self-consciously post-Christian Friends have hitherto thought possible. Above all, I have sought to describe, with passion and lucidity, the Quaker house, with its roaring fire, its library, and its expansive gardens. I want Friends to know that we can make our home in any part of the building, rather than limiting ourselves to a small number of rooms. I wish for Friends to feel absolutely at home in what belongs to them. It is my contention that we do a great disservice to our Quaker house when we warn each other to remain in one room only, or curtly inform one another that our excursions in the Quaker Way are under strict curfew. Whether these restrictions are imposed in the name of 'diversity' or the 'absolute perhaps', the impoverishment is the same. We lose nothing by exploring the older wings of our Quaker home. Indeed, we may discover hidden treasures sat gathering dust, neglected gems that we need in the present to beautify the mansion. If, after reading this book, a sizeable number of Friends still conclude that healthy Christian roots are superfluous to being Quaker today, at the very least, the present writer has attempted to articulate what such Friends may be leaving behind in the process. I have sought to remind Friends of our deep spiritual roots. The rest must be left to the dynamic process of tradition, in the act of returning again and again to the urgent question of who we are, and what we are doing here. If this book has made this conversation a little richer, it will have achieved its task. Let me conclude with an open invitation. The Quaker story is ours to tell. Let's start telling it.

Endnotes

1. Ben Pink Dandelion, *Open for Transformation: Being Quaker*, (London: Quaker Books, 2014), p. 54
2. Clifford Geertz, *The Interpretation of Cultures*, (New York: Basic Books, 1973), p. 20
3. Geertz, *The Interpretation of Cultures*, (New York: Basic Books, 1973), p. 18
4. Geertz, *The Interpretation of Cultures*, p. 6
5. Geertz, *The Interpretation of Cultures*, p. 89
6. Geertz, *The Interpretation* of Cultures, p. 95
7. Geertz, *The Interpretation of Cultures*, p. 24
8. George Whitehead, *The Light and Life of Christ Within ... the Quakers' Principles Justified*, (Philadelphia: Joseph Rakeshaw, 1668: 1823), p. 89
9. James Nayler, 'The Lamb's War against the Man of Sin', *Quaker Heritage Press*: http://www.qhpress.org/texts/nayler/lambswar.html [Accessed 7 January 2022]
10. William Evans & Thomas Evans, *Edward Burrough, A Memoir of a Faithful Servant of Christ, and Minister of the Gospel, who Died in Newgate*, 14th, 12 Mo., 1662), Charles Gulpin, 1851), p. 218
11. George Fox, *Gospel truth demonstrated, in a collection of doctrinal books, given forth by that faithful minister of Jesus Christ*, George Fox, Vol. III, (New York: Marcus T.C. Gould: 1831), p. 8
12. Fox, *Gospel truth demonstrated, in a collection of doctrinal books, given forth by that faithful minister of Jesus Christ*, George Fox, Vol. III, (New York: Marcus T.C. Gould: 1831), p. 9
13. George Fox, *The Journal*, ed. Nigel Smith, (London: Penguin Books, 1998), p. 27
14. Geertz, *The Interpretation of Cultures*, pp. 49–50

15. Simon Jenkins, "The Quakers are right. We don't need God", May 4th 2018, *The Guardian,* https://www.theguardian.com/commentisfree/2018/may/04/quakers-dropping-god

16. Jenkins, "The Quakers are right. We don't need God", May 4th 2018, *The Guardian*, https://www.theguardian.com/commentisfree/2018/may/04/quakers-dropping-god [Accessed March 27, 2022]

17. Letters: 'Debate on 'God language' doesn't mean all Quakers are losing faith', 7 May 2018, *The Guardian*, https://www.theguardian.com/world/2018/may/07/debate-on-god-language-doesnt-mean-all-quakers-are-losing-faith [Accessed March 27 2022]

18. Kevin Redfern, 'Doing Our Quaker Business', in *Searching the Depths: Essays in Search of Quaker Identity*, (London: Quaker Home Service, 1998), p. 77

19. David Boulton. 'Diversity', in *The Friend*, 9 April 2010, https://thefriend.org/article/letters-9-april-2010 [Accessed 18 May 2018]

20. Redfern, 'Doing Our Quaker Business', in *Searching the Depths: Essays in Search of Quaker Identity*, (London: Quaker Home Service, 1998), p. 83

21. Peter Tyler, *The Return of the Mystical: Ludwig Wittgenstein, Thresa of Avila, and the Christian Mystical Tradition*, (London: Continuum, 2011), p. 8

22. Rufus Jones, *Studies in Mystical Religion*, (London: Macmillan and Co, 1923), p. xxx

23. Rufus Jones, *The Later Period of Quakerism*, Volume I, (London, Macmillan, and Co, 1921), p. 5

24. Michael Birkel, *Quakers Reading Mystics, Quaker Studies*, (Leiden, Brill, 2018), p. 78

25. Jones, *Essential Writings,* ed. Kerry Walters, (New York: Orbis Books, 2001), p. 68

26. William Shewen, *Meditations and Experiences and Other Writings, MSF Early Quaker Series*, ed. Jason R. Henderson,

(CreateSpace Independent Publishing Platform, 2015), p. 112

27. Rufus Jones, 'Introduction', in William C. Braithwaite, *The Beginnings of Quakerism*, (London: Macmillan and Co, 1912), p. xiiii

28. Rufus Jones, *Essential Writings*, ed. Kerry Walters, (New York: Orbis Books, 2001), P. 77

29. Jones, *Essential Writings*, p. 58

30. Jones, *Essential Writings*, p. 141

31. Rufus Jones, *The Later Period of Quakerism, Volume I*, (London, Macmillan, and Co, 1921), p. 543

32. Birkel, *Quakers Reading Mystics, Quaker Studies*, (Leiden, Brill, 2018), p. 67

33. Jones, *Essential Writings,* p. 75

34. Jones, *Essential Writings*, p. ibid

35. Jones, *Essential Writings*, p. 49

36. Jones, *Essential Writings*, p. 89

37. Jones, *Essential Writings*, p. 119

38. Jones, *Essential Writings*, p. 88

39. Pink Dandelion, *Open for Transformation: The 2014 Swarthmore Lecture*, (London: Quaker Books, 2014), p. 47

40. Pink Dandelion, *Quakerism: An Introduction*, (Cambridge: Cambridge University Press, 2007), p. 134

41. Pink Dandelion, *Quakerism: An Introduction*, (Cambridge: Cambridge University Press, 2007), ibid

42. Rhiannon Grant, *British Quakerism and Religious Language*, (Leiden: Brill, 2018), p. 39

43. Grant, *British Quakerism and Religious Language*, (Leiden: Brill, 2018), p. 46

44. Grant, *British Quakerism and Religious Language*, p. 45

45. Grant, *British Quakerism and Religious Language*, (Leiden: Brill, 2018), p. 56

46. Tony Philpott, *From Christian to Quaker: A Spiritual Journey from Evangelical Christian to Universalist Quaker*, (Sarsen:

Quaker Universalist Publishing, 2013), p. 240

47. Philpott, *From Christian to Quaker: A Spiritual Journey from Evangelical Christian to Universalist Quaker*, (Sarsen: Quaker Universalist Publishing, 2013), p. ibid

48. Philpott, *From Christian to Quaker: A Spiritual Journey from Evangelical Christian to Universalist Quaker*, p. 237

49. Philpott, *From Christian to Quaker: A Spiritual Journey from Evangelical Christian to Universalist Quaker*, p. 246

50. The role of 'testimony' as the residual glue of a group that has otherwise given up shared expressions of faith, introduces us to an interesting fact concerning Liberal Quakerism's relationship to the past. Unable to produce stable forms from its individualised trajectories, Liberal Quakerism now draws upon language of an earlier theological tight-knit Quakerism to contain its radical diversity. Thus, the past is being used to authorise modernity, just as earlier Quakers looked back to the first generation to bolster ideas of proper Worship and discipline.

51. David Boulton, *The Faith of a Quaker Humanist*, (Torquay: Quaker Universalist Group, 1997), p. 17

52. Boulton, *The Faith of a Quaker Humanist*, (Torquay: Quaker Universalist Group, 1997), p. 17

53. Pink Dandelion, *Open for Transformation: Being Quaker*, (London: Quaker Books, 2014), p. 79

54. Rachel Muers, *Testimony: Quakerism and Theological Ethics*, (London: SCM Press, 2015), p. 22

55. Muers, *Testimony: Quakerism and Theological Ethics*, (London: SCM Press, 2015), p. 23

56. Muers, *Testimony: Quakerism and Theological Ethics*, pp. 23–4

57. Philpott, *From Christian to Quaker: A Spiritual Journey from Evangelical Christian to Universalist Quaker*, p. 246

58. Hannah Arendt, *The Life of the Mind*, (London: Harcourt, 1978), p. 15

59. Simon Best, 'The Religious Society of Friends in Britain:

Simple, Contemporary, Radical?', *The Friend,* May 2010, https://www.thefriend.co.uk/fq/082.pdf [Accessed 27 November 2021]

60. Best, 'The Religious Society of Friends in Britain: Simple, Contemporary, Radical?', *The Friend*, May 2010, https://www.thefriend.co.uk/fq/082.pdf [Accessed 27 November 2021]

61. Derek Guiton, *A Man Who Looks on Glass: Standing Up for God in the Religious Society of Friends, (Quakers),* (London: FeedARead Publishing, 2015), p. 221

62. Guiton, *A Man Who Looks on Glass: Standing Up for God in the Religious Society of Friends*, (Quakers), (London: FeedARead Publishing, 2015), p. 70

63. Guiton, *A Man Who Looks on Glass*, p. 58

64. Guiton, *A Man Who Looks on Glass*, p. 78

65. Guiton, *A Man Who Looks on Glass*, p. 14

66. Guiton, A Man Who Looks on Glass, p. 231

67. Guiton, *A Man Who Looks on Glass*, p. 232

68. Guiton, *A Man Who Looks on Glass*, p.13

69. Guiton, *A Man Who Looks on Glass*, pp. 13–4

70. Guiton, *A Man Who Looks on Glass*, p. 12

71. Guiton, *A Man Who Looks on Glass*, p. 55

72. Guiton, *A Man Who Looks on Glass*, p. 15

73. Guiton, *A Man Who Looks on Glass*, p. 75

74. Grant, *British Quakers and Religious Language*, p. 41

75. Guiton, *A Man Who Looks on Glass*, p. 71

76. George Fox, *The Journal of George Fox*, ed. Norman Penney, (New York: Cosimo, 2007), p.1

77. Fox, *The Journal of George Fox*, ed. Norman Penney, (New York: Cosimo, 2007), ibid

78. Richard Dean Smith, *The Middling Sort, and the Politics o Social Reformation: Colchester, 1570–1640,* (New York: Peter Lang, 2004), p. 92

79. Susan E. Schreiner, 'Creation and Providence', *The Calvin*

Handbook, ed. Herman J. Selderhuis, (Cambridge: Eerdmans Publishing Company, 2008), 274

80. Jean Calvin, *Institutes of the Christian Religion: Book first-Book second, chapter XI*, trans. Henry Beveridge, (London: Smith Elder and Co, 18445), p. 52

81. Calvin, *Institutes of the Christian Religion: Book first-Book second, chapter XI*, trans. Henry Beveridge, (London: Smith Elder and Co, 1845), p. 58

82. Nico Vorster, *The Brightest Mirror of God's Works: John Calvin's Theological Anthropology*, (Eugene: Pickwick Publications, 2019), p. 77

83. William C. Braithwaite, *The Beginnings of Quakerism*, (London: Macmillan & Co., 1912), p. 4

84. John Calvin, *Commentary on the Gospel According to John*, trans. William Pringle, (Woodstock: Devon Publishing, 2018), p. 21

85. Fox, *The Journal*, p. 2

86. Fox, *The Journal of George Fox*, p. 6

87. Jim Pym, *The Pure Principle: Quakers and Other Faith Traditions*, (York: The Ebor Press, 2000), p. 11

88. George Fox, *The Journal of George Fox: A Revised Edition*, ed. John L. Nickalis (Cambridge: Cambridge University Press, 2014), p. 33

89. Ludwig, Wittgenstein, *Culture and Value*, trans Peter Winch, (Oxford: Basil Blackwell, 1977), p. 28e

90. George Fox, *A collection of many select and Christian epistles, letters, and testimonies, written on sundry occasions, by that ancient, eminent, faithful Friend and minister of Christ Jesus*, (New York: Marcus T.C. Gould, 1831), p. 332

91. Margret Fell quoted in Muers, *Testimony*, p. 36

92. Fox, *The Journal of George Fox*, p. 17

93. Fox, *The Journal of George Fox*, ibid

94. Jean *Calvin, Institutes of the Christian religion*, trans Henry Beveridge, (Edinburgh: T&T Clark, 1863), p. 14

95. See Michael P. Winship, *Hot Protestants: A History of Puritanism in England and America*, (New Haven: Yale University Press, 2019), p. 11

96. David D. Hall, *The Puritans: A Transatlantic History*, (Princeton: Princeton University Press, 2021), p. 15

97. Carla Geron, *Night Journeys: The Power of Dreams in Transatlantic Quaker Culture*, (London: University of Virginian Press, 2004), p. 56

98. Fox, *A collection of many select and Christian epistles, letters, and testimonies, written on sundry occasions, by that ancient, eminent, faithful Friend and minister of Christ Jesus*, (New York: Marcus T.C. Gould, 1831), p. 235

99. See Quakers, *Creation Care, and Sustainability: Quakers and the Disciplines: Volume 6*, ed. Cherice Bock, Stephen Potthoff, Rebecca Artinian-Kaiser et al, (Longmeadow: Full Media Services, 2019)

100. Wittgenstein, *Culture and Value*, trans Peter Winch, (Oxford: Basil Blackwell, 1977), p. 50c

101. Stanley Hauerwas, *Hannah's Child: A Theologian's Memoir*, (London: SCM Press, 2010), p. X

102. God, Words and Us: Quakers in Conversation about Religious Difference, ed. Helen Rowlands (London: Quaker Books, 2017), pp. 63–4

103. Rudolf Bultmann, 'New Testament and Theology: The Problem of Demythologising the New Testament Proclamation', in *Mythology and the New Testament and Other Basic Writings*, trans. Schubert M. Ogden, (Minneapolis: Fortress Press, 1984), pp. 4–5

104. Fox, *The Journal of George Fox: A Revised Edition*, ed. John L. Nickalis, (Cambridge: Cambridge University Press, 2014), p. 346

105. Quoted in James Mullaney, *Celebrating the Universe! The Spirituality & Science of Stargazing*, (London: Hay House, 2013), p. 165

106. Wittgenstein, *Culture and Value*, p. 33e

107. *Quaker Faith and Practice*, 5th Edition, 19.08

108. As Boulton writes: '[He] did turn water into wine, did raise Lazarus from the dead, did teach that we should love our enemies, was crucified, and buried, did descend into hell, did rise again, and did ascend into heaven. We can demonstrate that all these things really do happen, just as we can show that Hamlet really does see his father's ghost, and Frodo Baggins really does succeed in destroying the ring in the Crack of Doom', in *The Trouble with God: Religious Humanism and the Republic of Heaven*, (Alresford: John Hunt Publishing, 2002), p. 187

109. John Greenleaf Whittier, *The Letters, Vol. III*, ed. John B. Pickard, (London: Harvard University Press, 1975), p. 222

110. *Quaker Faith and Practice*, 19.28

111. George Fox, Epistle 388, quoted in Pink Dandelion, *Quakers: A Short Introduction*, (Oxford: Oxford University Press, 2008), p. 88

112. Numbers 22:41–23: 12 41

113. Isaiah 45: 1–7

114. Lewis Benson, 'The Christian Universalism of George Fox', *The New Foundation Fellowship*: http://storage.ning.com/topology/rest/1.0/file/get/1115043257?profile=original [Accessed, 16 December 2021]

115. Doug Gwyn, *Apocalypse of the Word: The Life and Message of George Fox*, (Richmond: Friends Unity Press, 1986), p. 88

116. Janet Scott, *What Canst Thou Say: Towards a Quaker Theology*, (London: Quaker Books, 1980: 2007), p. 53

117. Shewen, *Meditations and Experiences and Other Writings, MSF Early Quaker Series*, ed. Jason R. Henderson, (CreateSpace Independent Publishing Platform, 2015), p. 82

118. Richard Barnes, 'From the Clerk', in *Universalism and Spirituality*, ed. Patricia A. Williams, (Columbia: The Quaker Universalist Fellowship, 2007), p. 107

119. Gene Kudsen Hoffman, 'Jesus, The Christ, Quakers and I', in *Universalism and Spirituality*, ed. Patricia A. Williams, (Columbia: The Quaker Universalist Fellowship, 2007), p. 97

120. William Penn, 'Advice to his Children, Chapter 3', *The Quaker Writings Home Page*, http://www.qhpress.org/quakerpages/qwhp/advice3.htm (Accessed 17 Dec. 21)

121. William Penn, *Select Works of William Penn. To which is prefixed a journal of his life: Volume 1*, (London: William Philips), p. 548

122. Karl Barth, *On Religion*, trans. Garrett Green, (London: T&T Clark, 2006), p. 58

123. Barth, *On Religion*, trans. Garrett Green, (London: T&T Clark, 2006), p.86

124. Barth, *On Religion*, ibid

125. Barth, *On Religion*, p. 65

126. Barth, *On Religion*, p. 86

127. Robert Barclay, *An Apology for the True Christian Divinity, Being an Explanation and Vindication of the Principles and Doctrines of the Quakers*, (London: John Baskerville, 1765), p. 95

128. This fact is expressed with equal power in Paul's recorded preaching among the Athenians, (Acts 17:22–31). At the centre of Paul's evangelical exposition is the notion of the 'unknown god'. This shadowy presence is intended to draw the hearers into the thought-world of the Gospel. In his speech, Paul draws his listeners into the realm they know in order to subvert their knowledge. First Paul speaks in the accent of the Stoic poet Aratus: '"For in him we live and move and have our being." As some of your own poets have said, "We are his offspring." Therefore since we are God's offspring, we should not think that the divine being is like gold or silver or stone — an image made by human design and skill' (17:28–9). Here the author of Acts shows Paul

using the Stoic conception of the transcendent Fatherhood of God as a 'hook', to draw his audience into the strange kerygma of Jesus Christ. Having established the divine life through the imagination of Greek paganism, Paul goes on to describe the activity of God's Son: 'For he has set a day when he will judge the world with justice by the man he has appointed. He has given proof of this to everyone by raising him from the dead' (NIV 17:30).

129. Clive Staples Lewis, *The Essential C.S. Lewis*, (London: Scribner, 2017), p. 56

130. Allen, *Ground and Spring: Foundations of Quaker discipleship*, (London: Quaker Books, 2007), pp. 100–1

131. Allen, Ground and Spring: Foundations of Quaker discipleship, p. 113

132. Allen, *Ground and Spring: Foundations of Quaker discipleship*, ibid

133. Emmanuel Levinas, *Entre Nous: Essays on Thinking-of-the-Other*, trans. Michael Smith & Barbara Harshaw, (New York: Columbia University Press, 1998), p. 230

134. Allen, *Ground and Spring: Foundations of Quaker discipleship*, (London: Quaker Books, 2007), p. 99

135. This problem of 'Quaker seriousness' confronts us with a fundamental matter concerning the proper valuation of self-denial. Centuries of pious exhortation have taught us to despise the little things of life and regard simple pleasure with utmost disdain But the best among the Humanists are closer to the ethic of Jesus when they insist that there is something akin to secular holiness in the pleasures of the present moment, especially if it makes us tender towards one another. This lesson is powerfully illustrated in the Gospel of John's account of Mary's anointing of Jesus: 'Mary took about a pint of pure nard, an expensive perfume; she poured it on Jesus' feet and wiped his feet with her hair. And the house was filled with the fragrance

of the perfume. But one of his disciples, Judas Iscariot, who was later to betray him, objected, "Why wasn't this perfume sold and the money given to the poor? It was worth a year's wages…" "Leave her alone," Jesus replied. "It was intended that she should save this perfume for the day of my burial. You will always have the poor among you, but you will not always have me"' (NIV John 12:3–7). In this provocative scene, Mary's act of extravagance is authorized by Jesus despite its seeming carelessness in a culture of extreme scarcity. The implication of this passage is that deep love and personal attachment justifies the offering of a gift, even if it appears wasteful. Here, Jesus emerges as a robust sanctifier of the libidinal principle of pleasure for pleasure's sake, while Judas appears as the perverse spokesman of shallow purity, who forgets that religiosity is about the care of real human beings standing before us and not showy, holier-than-thou principles of asceticism.

136. E.M. Forster, 'What I Believe', in *Two Cheers for Democracy*, (Harmondsworth: Penguin, 1951: 1965), p. 83

137. Thomas R. Kelly, *Testament of Devotion*, (New York: HarperCollins Publishing, 1992), pp. 66–7

138. Julian of Norwich, *Revelations of Divine Love*, (London: Penguin Books, 1998), p. 114

139. Jonathan Head, *The Philosophy of Anne Conway: God, Creation, and the Nature of Time*, (London: Bloomsbury Publishing, 2020), p. 3

140. Francesco La Nave, 'The Central Role of Suffering in Anne Conway's Philosophy', *Bruniana & Campanelliana*, 2006, Vol. 12, No. 1 (2006), p.181

141. T. L. Underwood, 'Sir John Finch and the Viscountess Anne Conway: Two Unpublished Letters, *Quaker History, Autumn 1978, Vol. 67, No. 2* (Autumn 1978), p. 116

142. Quoted in John Henry, 'A Cambridge Platonist's

Materialism: Henry More and the Concept of Soul', *Journal of the Warburg and Courtauld Institutes*, 1986, Vol. 49 (1986), p. 176

143. Hannah Newton, *The Sick Child in Early Modern England, 1580-1720,* (Oxford: Oxford University Press, 2012), p. 150

144. Donald Worster, *Nature's Economy: A History of Ecological Ideas*, (Cambridge: Cambridge University, 1994), p. 42

145. Jasper Reid, The Metaphysics of Henry More, (London: Springer Netherlands, 2012), p. 264

146. Henry More, 'The Dream of Bathynous', in *English Prose, Vol. II. Sixteenth Century to the Restoration*, ed. Henry Craik, (New York: The Macmillan Company, 1916), p. 13; Bartleby. com, 2010. www.bartleby.com/209/ [Accessed 29 Dec. 21]

147. Anne Conway, *The Principles of the Most Ancient and Modern Philosophy*, trans. Alison P. Coudert, (Cambridge: Cambridge University Press, 1996), pp. 44–5

148. David Byrne, 'Ragley Hall and the Decline of Cartesianism', *Restoration: Studies in English Literary Culture, 1660-1700*, Vol. 40, No. 2 (Fall 2016), p. 43

149. Anne Conway & Henry More, *Conway Letters: The Correspondence of Anne,* ed. Marjorie Hope Nicolson, (Yale: Yale University Press, 1930), p. 422

150. Conway & More, *Conway Letters,* ed. Marjorie Hope Nicolson, (Yale: Yale University Press, 1930), p. 439

151. Conway, *The Principles of the Most Ancient and Modern Philosophy*, trans. Alison P. Coudert, (Cambridge: Cambridge University Press, 1996), p. 32

152. Conway, *The Principles* p. 37

153. Conway, *The Principles*, p. 31

154. Conway, *The Principles*, p. 61

155. Conway, *The Principles*, p. 42

156. Plotinus, 'Providence': First Treatise', in *The Enneads*, trans. Stephen McKenna, (London: Penguin Books, 1991), p. 155

157. Conway, *The Principles*, p. 27

158. Conway, *The Principles*, p. 43

159. Conway, *The Principles*, ibid

160. Conway, *The Principles*, p. 23

161. Plotinus, 'On the Good, or The One', in *The Enneads,* trans. Stephen McKenna, (London: Penguin Books, 1991), p. 549

162. In his treatise 'On Prayer', the third-century theologian Origen writes: 'Nay more, beholding ever the face of the Father in heaven and looking on the Godhead of our Creator, the angel of each man, even of "little ones" within the church, both prays with us, and acts with us where possible, for the objects of our prayer'. Trans. William A. Curtis, *Early Church Fathers*, Nottingham Publishing, 2008: https://www.tertullian.org/fathers/origen_on_prayer_02_text.htm [Accessed 01/01/2022]

163. Conway, *The Principles*, p.62

164. Conway, *The Principles,* p. 35

165. Owen Davies, *Popular Magic: Cunning-folk in English History*, (London: Continuum: 2007), p. 37

166. Conway, *The Principles,* p. 59

167. Conway, *The Principles*, p. 35

168. Conway, *The Principles*, p. 42

169. See, Jeffrey Burton Russell, *Satan: The Early Christian Tradition*, (New York: Cornwell University Press, 1987), p. 145

170. Conway, *The Principles*, p. 39

171. Conway, *The Principles*, p. 17

172. Conway, *The Principles*, ibid

173. See *The Impact of the Kabbalah in the Seventeenth Century: The Life and Thought of Francis Mercury Van Helmont (1614– 1698),* (Lieden: Brill, 1999), p. 250

174. Sarah Hutton, *Anne Conway: A Woman Philosopher*, (Cambridge: Cambridge University Press, 2004), p. 226

175. Conway, *The Principles*, p. 13

176. Gerald Hewitson, *Journey into Life: Inheriting the Story of*

Early Friends, (London: Quaker Books, 2013), p. 37

177. Hewitson, *Journey into Life: Inheriting the Story of Early Friends*, (London: Quaker Books, 2013), ibid

178. Hewitson, *Journey into Life: Inheriting the Story of Early Friends*, p. 38

179. Charles Taylor, *A Secular Age*, (London: Harvard University Press, 2007), p. 39

180. Conway, *The Principles*, p. 64

181. Conway, *The Principles*, ibid

182. Conway, *The Principles*, p. 64

183. Conway, *The Principles*, p. 63

184. Taylor, *A Secular Age*, (London: Harvard University Press, 2007), p. 284

185. Conway, *The Principles*, p. 70

186. Origen, *On First Principles*, trans. G.W. Butterworth, (Notre Dame: Christian Classics, 2013), p. 331

187. Origen, *On First Principles*, p. 330

188. Origen, *On First Principles*, p. 328

189. Hutton, *Anne Conway: A Woman Philosopher*, (Cambridge: Cambridge University Press, 2004), p. 71

190. Panagiōtēs Tzamalikos, *Origen: Philosophy of History & Eschatology*, (Leiden: Brill, 2007), p. 50

191. Carl Séan O'Brien, *The Demiurge in Ancient Thought: Secondary Gods and Divine Mediators*, (Cambridge: Cambridge University Press, 2015), p. 287

192. See Anthony C. Thiselton, *Systematic Theology*, (Cambridge: William B. Eerdmans Publishing Company), p. 117

193. Conway, *The Principles*, p. 34

194. Conway, *The Principles*, p. 35

195. Conway, *The Principles*, p. 31

196. Conway, *The Principles*, p. 31

197. Albert Schweitzer, *Civilization and Ethics*, (London: Adam & Charles Black, 1949), p. 245

198. Schweitzer, *Civilization and Ethics*, (London: Adam &

Charles Black, 1949), p. 245

199. Schweitzer, *Civilization and Ethics*, p. 241

200. Schweitzer, *Civilization and Ethics*, p. 248

201. Schweitzer, *Civilization and Ethics*, p. 241

202. Schweitzer, *Civilization and Ethics*, p. 242

203. Schweitzer, *Civilization and Ethics*, p. 245

204. Conway, *The Principles*, p. 38

205. Schweitzer, *Civilization and Ethics*, p. 248

206. Alasdair MacIntyre, *After Virtue: A Study in Moral Theory*, (London: Bloomsbury,2007), p. 257

207. Homer, *The Odyssey*, trans. D.C.H. Rieu, (Penguin Books, 1991), pp. 108–109

208. See *The Broadview Anthology of British Literature Volume 6A: The Twentieth Century and Beyond: From 1900 to Mid Century, Volume 6*, ed. Anne Lake Prescott, Barry V. Qualls, Claire Waters et al. (New York: Broadview Press, 2008), p. 463

References

Allen, Beth, *Ground and Spring: Foundations of Quaker discipleship*, (London: Quaker Books, 2007)

Arendt, Hannah, *The Life of the Mind*, (London: Harcourt, 1978)

Barclay, Robert, *An Apology for the True Christian Divinity, Being an Explanation and Vindication of the Principles and Doctrines of the Quakers*, (London: John Baskerville, 1765)

Barnes, Richard, 'From the Clerk', in *Universalism and Spirituality*, ed. Patricia A. Williams, (Columbia: The Quaker Universalist Fellowship, 2007)

Barth, Karl, *On Religion*, trans. Garrett Green, (London: T&T Clark, 2006)

Benson, Lewis, 'The Christian Universalism of George Fox', *The New Foundation Fellowship:* http://storage.ning.com/topology/rest/1.0/file/get/1115043257?profile=original (Accessed, 16 December 2021)

Best, Simon, 'The Religious Society of Friends in Britain: Simple, Contemporary, Radical?', *The Friend,* May 2010, https://www.thefriend.co.uk/fq/082.pdf [Accessed 27 November 2021]

Birkel, Michael, *Quakers Reading Mystics, Quaker Studies*, (Leiden, Brill, 2018)

Boulton, David, Boulton, David, *The Faith of a Quaker Humanist*, (Torquay: Quaker Universalist Group, 1997)

Boulton, David, 'Diversity', in The Friend, 9 April 2010, https://thefriend.org/article/letters-9-april-2010 [Accessed 18 May 2018]

Boulton, David, *The Trouble with God: Religious Humanism and the Republic of Heaven*, (Alresford: John Hunt Publishing, 2002)

Bultmann, Rudolf, 'New Testament and Theology: The Problem of Demythologising the New Testament Proclamation', in *Mythology and the New Testament and Other Basic Writings*, trans. Schubert M. Ogden, (Minneapolis: Fortress Press, 1984)

Burton Russell, Jeffrey, *Satan: The Early Christian Tradition*, (New York: Cornwell University Press, 1987)

Braithwaite, William C., *The Beginnings of Quakerism*, (London: Macmillan and Co, 1912)

Byrne, David, 'Ragley Hall and the Decline of Cartesianism', Restoration: Studies in English Literary Culture, 1660–1700, Vol. 40, No. 2 (Fall 2016)

Calvin, Jean, *Institutes of the Christian Religion: Book first-Book second, chapter XI*, trans. Henry Beveridge, (London: Smith Elder and Co, 1845)

Calvin, Jean, *Institutes of the Christian religion*, trans Henry Beveridge, (Edinburgh: T&T Clark, 1863)

Calvin, Jen, *Commentary on the Gospel According to John*, trans. William Pringle, (Woodstock: Devon Publishing, 2018)

Conway, *The Principles of the Most Ancient and Modern Philosophy*, trans. Alison P. Coudert, (Cambridge: Cambridge University Press, 1996)

Conway Anne, & More Henry, Conway Letters: The Correspondence of Anne, ed. Marjorie Hope Nicolson, (Yale: Yale University Press, 1930)

Coudert, Alison, *The Impact of the Kabbalah in the Seventeenth Century: The Life and Thought of Francis Mercury Van Helmont (1614–1698)*, (Lieden: Brill, 1999)

Dandelion, Ben Pink, *Quakerism: An Introduction*, (Cambridge: Cambridge University Press, 2007

Dandelion, Ben Pink, *Quakers: A Short Introduction*, (Oxford: Oxford University Press, 2008)

Dandelion, Ben Pink, *Open for Transformation: Being Quaker,* (London: Quaker Books, 2014)

Davies, Owen, *Popular Magic: Cunning-folk in English History,* (London: Continuum: 2007)

Eliot, T.S., *The Four Quartets,* quoted in *The Broadview Anthology of British Literature Volume 6A: The Twentieth Century and Beyond: From 1900 to Mid Century, Volume 6,* ed. Anne Lake

Prescott, Barry V. Qualls, Claire Waters et al. (New York: Broadview Press, 2008)

Forster, E.M. 'What I Believe', in *Two Cheers for Democracy*, (Harmondsworth: Penguin, 1951: 1965)

Fox, George, *A collection of many select and Christian epistles, letters, and testimonies, written on sundry occasions, by that ancient, eminent, faithful Friend and minister of Christ Jesus,* (New York: Marcus T.C. Gould, 1831)

Fox, George, *The Journal of George Fox: A Revised Edition,* ed. John L. Nickalis (Cambridge: Cambridge University Press, 2014)

Fox, George, *The Journal of George Fox,* ed. Norman Penney, (New York: Cosimo, 2007)

Geron, Carla, *Night Journeys: The Power of Dreams in Transatlantic Quaker Culture,* (London: University of Virginian Press, 2004)

Guiton, Derek, *A Man Who Looks on Glass: Standing Up for God in the Religious Society of Friends,* (Quakers), (London: FeedARead Publishing, 2015)

Guiton, Derek, *God, Words and Us: Quakers in Conversation about Religious Difference,* ed. Helen Rowlands, (London: Quaker Books, 2017)

Grant, Rhiannon, *British Quakerism and Religious Language,* (Leiden: Brill, 2018)

Greenleaf Whittier, John, *The Letters, Vol. III,* ed. John B. Pickard, (London: Harvard University Press, 1975)

Gwyn, Douglas, *Apocalypse of the Word: The Life and Message of George Fox,* (Richmond: Friends Unity Press, 1986)

Head, Jonathan, *The Philosophy of Anne Conway: God, Creation, and the Nature of Time,* (London: Bloomsbury Publishing, 2020)

Hall, David D., *The Puritans: A Transatlantic History,* (Princeton: Princeton University Press, 2021)

Hauerwas, Stanley, *Hannah's Child: A Theologian's Memoir,* (London: SCM Press, 2010)

Henry, John, 'A Cambridge Platonist's Materialism: Henry More and the Concept of Soul', *Journal of the Warburg and Courtauld Institutes*, 1986, Vol. 49 (1986)

Hewitson, Gerald, *Journey into Life: Inheriting the Story of Early Friends*, (London: Quaker Books, 2013)

Hoffman, Gene Kudsen, 'Jesus, The Christ, Quakers and I', in *Universalism and Spirituality*, ed. Patricia A. Williams, (Columbia: The Quaker Universalist Fellowship, 2007)

Homer, *The Odyssey*, trans. D.C.H. Rieu, (Penguin Books, 1991)

Hutton, Sarah, *Anne Conway: A Woman Philosopher*, (Cambridge: Cambridge University Press, 2004)

Jones, Rufus *The Later Period of Quakerism, Volume I*, (London, Macmillan, and Co, 1921)

Jones, Rufus, *Studies in Mystical Religion*, (London: Macmillan and Co, 1923)

Jones, Rufus, *Essential Writings*, ed. Kerry Walters, (New York: Orbis Books, 2001)

Jenkins, Simon, "The Quakers are right. We don't need God", May 4th, 2018, *The Guardian*, https://www.theguardian.com/commentisfree/2018/may/04/quakers-dropping-god

Kelly, Thomas R., *Testament of Devotion,* (New York: HarperCollins Publishing, 1992)

La Nave, Francesco, 'The Central Role of Suffering in Anne Conway's Philosophy', *Bruniana & Campanelliana*, 2006, Vol. 12, No. 1 (2006)

Letters: 'Debate on 'God language' doesn't mean all Quakers are losing faith', 7 May 2018, *The Guardian*, https://www.theguardian.com/world/2018/may/07/debate-on-god-language-doesnt-mean-all-quakers-are-losing-faith

Levinas, Emmanuel, *Entre Nous: Essays on Thinking-of-the-Other*, trans. Michael Smith & Barbara Harshaw, (New York: Columbia University Press, 1998)

Lewis, Clive Staples, *The Essential C.S. Lewis*, (London: Scribner, 2017)

MacIntyre, Alasdair, *After Virtue: A Study in Moral Theory*,

(London: Bloomsbury, 2007)

More, Henry, 'The Dream of Bathynous', in *English Prose, Vol. II. Sixteenth Century to the Restoration*, ed. Henry Craik (New York: The Macmillan Company, 1916), Bartleby.com, 2010, www.bartleby.com/209/ [Accessed 29 Dec. 21].

Mullaney, James, *Celebrating the Universe! The Spirituality & Science of Stargazing*, (London: Hay House, 2013)

Muers, Rachel, *Testimony: Quakerism and Theological Ethics*, (London: SCM Press, 2015)

Newton, Hannah, *The Sick Child in Early Modern England, 1580–1720,* (Oxford: Oxford University Press, 2012)

Norwich, Julian of, *Revelations of Divine Love*, (London: Penguin Books, 1998)

O'Brien, Carl Séan, *The Demiurge in Ancient Thought: Secondary Gods and Divine Mediators*, (Cambridge: Cambridge University Press, 2015)

Origen, *On First Principles*, trans. G.W. Butterworth, (Notre Dame: Christian Classics, 2013)

Origen, 'On Prayer', trans. William A. Curtis, *Early Church Fathers*, (Nottingham Publishing, 2008)

Penn, William, 'Advice to his Children, Chapter 3', The Quaker Writings Home Page, http://www.qhpress.org/quakerpages/qwhp/advice3.htm (Accessed 17 Dec. 21)

Select Works of William Penn. To which is prefixed a journal of his life: Volume 1, (London: William Philips, 1825)

Philpott, Tony, *From Christian to Quaker: A Spiritual Journey from Evangelical Christian to Universalist Quaker*, (Sarsen: Quaker Universalist Publishing, 2013)

Plotinus, *The Enneads*, trans. Stephen McKenna, (London: Penguin Books, 1991)

Pym, Jim, *The Pure Principle: Quakers and Other Faith Traditions*, (York: The Ebor Press, 2000)

Quakers, Creation Care, and Sustainability: Quakers and the Disciplines: Volume 6, ed. Cherice Bock, Stephen Potthoff,

Rebecca Artinian-Kaiser et al, (Longmeadow: Full Media Services, 2019)

Quaker Faith and Practice, 5th Edition, (London: Religious Society of Friends, 1995: 2022)

Redfern, Kevin, 'Doing Our Quaker Business', in *Searching the Depths: Essays in Search of Quaker Identity,* (London: Quaker Home Service, 1998)

Reid, Jasper, *The Metaphysics of Henry More,* (London: Springer Netherlands, 2012

Schreiner, Susan E., 'Creation and Providence', *The Calvin Handbook,* ed. Herman J. Selderhuis, (Cambridge: Eerdmans Publishing Company, 2008)

Shewen, William, *Meditations and Experiences and Other Writings, MSF Early Quaker Series,* ed. Jason R. Henderson, (CreateSpace Independent Publishing Platform, 2015)

Scott, Janet, *What Canst Thou Say: Towards a Quaker Theology,* (London: Quaker Books, 1980: 2007)

Schweitzer, *Civilization and Ethics,* (London: Adam & Charles Black, 1949)

Smith, Richard, Dean, *The Middling Sort, and the Politics of Social Reformation: Colchester, 1570–1640,* (New York: Peter Lang, 2004)

Taylor, Charles, *A Secular Age,* (London: Harvard University Press, 2007)

Thiselton, Anthony C., *Systematic Theology,* (Cambridge: William B. Eerdmans Publishing Company)

Tyler, Peter, *The Return of the Mystical: Ludwig Wittgenstein, Thresa of Avila, and the Christian Mystical Tradition,* (London: Continuum, 2011)

Tzamalikos, Panagiōtēs, *Origen: Philosophy of History & Eschatology,* (Leiden: Brill, 2007)

Underwood, T.L., 'Sir John Finch and the Viscountess Anne Conway: Two Unpublished Letters' *Quaker History,* Autumn 1978, Vol. 67, No. 2 (Autumn 1978)

Vorster, Nico, *The Brightest Mirror of God's Works: John Calvin's Theological Anthropology*, (Eugene: Pickwick Publications, 2019)

Worster, Donald, *Nature's Economy: A History of Ecological Ideas*, (Cambridge: Cambridge University, 1994

Wittgenstein, Ludwig, *Culture and Value*, trans Peter Winch, (Oxford: Basil Blackwell, 1977)

Winship, Michael P., *Hot Protestants: A History of Puritanism in England and America*, (New Haven: Yale University Press, 2019)

Further Reading

Allen, Beth, *Ground and Spring: Foundations of Quaker discipleship*, Quaker Books, 2007

Barnett, Craig, *The Guided Life: Finding purpose in troubled times*, Christian Alternative Books, 2019

Dandelion, Ben, Pink, *Living the Quaker way*, Quaker Books. 2019

Daniels, C. Wess, *A Convergent Model of Renewal: Remixing the Quaker Tradition in a Participatory Culture*, Pickwick Publications, 2015

Gwyn, Douglas, *The Covenant Crucified*, Quaker Books, 2006

Hauerwas, Stanley, *The Peaceable Kingdom: A Primer in Christian Ethics*, University of Notre Dame Press, 1991

Muers, Rachel, *Testimony: Quakerism and Theological Ethics*, 2015

Ohio Yearly Meeting, *Traditional Quaker Christianity*, Rabbit Press, 2014

Russ, Mark, *Quaker-Shaped Christianity: How the Jesus Story and the Quaker Way fit Together*, Christian Alternative Books, 2021

Wilson, Lloyd, Lee, *Essays on the Quaker Vision of Gospel Order*, Quaker Press of Friends General, 2002

CHRISTIAN ALTERNATIVE
BOOKS

THE NEW OPEN SPACES

Throughout the two thousand years of Christian tradition there
have been, and still are, groups and individuals that exist in
the margins and upon the edge of faith. But in Christianity's
contrapuntal history it has often been these outcasts and
pioneers that have forged contemporary orthodoxy out
of former radicalism as belief evolves to engage with and
encompass the ever-changing social and scientific realities. Real
faith lies not in the comfortable certainties of the Orthodox,
but somewhere in a half-glimpsed hinterland on the dirt track
to Emmaus, where the Death of God meets the Resurrection,
where the supernatural Christ meets the historical Jesus,
and where the revolution liberates both the oppressed and
the oppressors.
Welcome to Christian Alternative... a space at the edge where
the light shines through.
If you have enjoyed this book, why not tell other readers by
posting a review on your preferred book site.

Recent bestsellers from Christian Alternative are:

Bread Not Stones
The Autobiography of An Eventful Life
Una Kroll
The spiritual autobiography of a truly remarkable woman
and a history of the struggle for ordination in the Church of
England.
Paperback: 978-1-78279-804-0 ebook: 978-1-78279-805-7

The Quaker Way
A Rediscovery
Rex Ambler
Although fairly well known, Quakerism is not well understood.
The purpose of this book is to explain how Quakerism works as
a spiritual practice.
Paperback: 978-1-78099-657-8 ebook: 978-1-78099-658-5

Blue Sky God
The Evolution of Science and Christianity
Don MacGregor
Quantum consciousness, morphic fields and blue-sky
thinking about God and Jesus the Christ.
Paperback: 978-1-84694-937-1 ebook: 978-1-84694-938-8

Celtic Wheel of the Year
Tess Ward
An original and inspiring selection of prayers combining
Christian and Celtic Pagan traditions, and interweaving their
calendars into a single pattern of prayer for every morning
and night of the year.
Paperback: 978-1-90504-795-6

Christian Atheist
Belonging without Believing
Brian Mountford
Christian Atheists don't believe in God but miss him: especially
the transcendent beauty of his music, language, ethics, and
community.
Paperback: 978-1-84694-439-0 ebook: 978-1-84694-929-6

Compassion Or Apocalypse?
A Comprehensible Guide to the Thoughts of René Girard
James Warren
How René Girard changes the way we think about God and the
Bible, and its relevance for our apocalypse-threatened world.
Paperback: 978-1-78279-073-0 ebook: 978-1-78279-072-3

Diary Of A Gay Priest
The Tightrope Walker
Rev. Dr. Malcolm Johnson
Full of anecdotes and amusing stories, but the Church is still a
dangerous place for a gay priest.
Paperback: 978-1-78279-002-0 ebook: 978-1-78099-999-9

Do You Need God?
Exploring Different Paths to Spirituality Even For Atheists
Rory J.Q. Barnes
An unbiased guide to the building blocks of spiritual belief.
Paperback: 978-1-78279-380-9 ebook: 978-1-78279-379-3

Readers of ebooks can buy or view any of these bestsellers by clicking on the live link in the title. Most titles are published in paperback and as an ebook. Paperbacks are available in traditional bookshops. Both print and ebook formats are available online.

Find more titles and sign up to our readers' newsletter at
http://www.johnhuntpublishing.com/christianity
Follow us on Facebook at
https://www.facebook.com/ChristianAlternative